the ARtrepreneur

Financial Success for Artistic Souls

To Darren
thank you for the
magic & inspiration!
x

Evelyne Brink

Published by Papy Publishing
1 Redwood Mews, London SW4 0LJ

ISBN 978-0-9570988-0-0

Illustrations by Evelyne Brink
Design and layout by impact studios

This book is for the wonderful people on this planet who believe in the importance of creativity.

I dedicate this book to you.

To the people who said I couldn't write a book in my 3rd language: the earth is no longer flat.

To the people who always believed I'd do it: You were so right.

Thank you Paul Copeland, who came up with the title- we wanted to get it right.

This book started out as " The Money Mindset makeover for Artistic Souls" which was too lengthy- well no one could remember it. They'd say "the book you're writing about money"- I wanted something more snappy and to the point. So I set out a little competition and Paul found just the right term: The Artrepreneur.

I'm so happy with that. Turns out the years on the stand up comedy circuit came in useful (for both of us).

Thank you Arvind Devalia for your kind support and guidance. You've been incredibly helpful.

Thank you to all my challenges that helped me become the person I am today.

Thanks to Michael Neill for inspiring, coaching and guiding my thinking since 2005.

To Rich Litvin for deep coaching and without whom my business wouldn't be what it is today.

To Steve Chandler, whose work has liberated my mind and soul.

Thank you, Robert Holden for your wonderful feedback on the book. That has really lifted me up.

Thank you to all my clients for being the coolest people in the world and for allowing me the pleasure of coaching you. I am so proud of every one of you.

Thank you for my friends whose questions and care kept me going.

Thanks to my sister Jessica, who patiently listened to the earliest draft in the car without falling asleep at the wheels despite being pregnant and the draft at times being a bit daft. But though it shouldn't have you fall asleep, please don't read this book whilst driving. I'll make you an audio version.

Thanks to my Dad for all his smart sayings which came in very handy and to my Mum for her unbridled enthusiasm, love and presence.

Thank you to my beloved Thomas for being the most loving, supportive and amazing man I could have wished for. I am so happy to grow with you in love and to finally start our family. I love you so much.

And to our son: You'll be born soon after this book. It's during your coming into this world that a lot of the work on this was done, thank you for having me sit still for so long so I could actually get on with it. I have a feeling the sitting still part might be over once you're here? I love you very much.

Introduction

MONEY

is better than
poverty, if only
for financial
reasons.

Woody Allen

Let's say you're not a born business person. Let's assume you're not one for picking up books about how to make money. Because you've got a life and many interests beyond getting rich. But you do wonder:

How does this money thing work? And: Do I care? Yes, I care. No, I don't. Yes, I do. No, I don't. Well, actually I do.

Through the years of working with the most talented people in this world – Artistic Souls with big hearts and high ethics – I've noticed that question has been the common denominator. It troubles everyone, causing sleepless nights, stress and desperation.

People tend to think in two categories: you're either a business person or an artist type. You're either good with money or not. You're good at either maths or languages.

It's easy to see that this doesn't hold up to the truth. There are great business people who are artistic, and great artists who know about business. There are people who are good with money, others are bad – and the most extraordinary news is that we are all able to learn.

We don't have to make do with what we know today. We don't have to settle for what we've got. We don't have to keep ourselves trapped in our own minds.

There is more to life than shoes. There is more to being creative than struggling and getting high. There is more to success than being a millionaire.

I wrote this book for the open-hearted imaginative type of people who want fun ways to understand money and how to make it, keep it, spend it and invest it. We will be talking about authentic success: that is, doing what you really want, knowing why you do it and living an inspired life. In this world we need money to weave our tapestry of creations so I will clear away the cobwebs of those scary old money stories that hang around like old ghosts frightening the hell out of this world's most beautiful souls. Yes, I'm talking about you!

> ***I am attempting something huge: an abundance revolution for Artistic Souls. For centuries artistry has been closely linked to struggle – of both a personal and a financial nature.***

I want to liberate all the creative-minded and offer up a new mindset shift to abundance as our primary source of inspiration. I am inviting you to create the life you were born to live.

This way of living I call being an Artrepreneur. A free spirit creating a happy living with your heart and Artistic Soul.

How I got there in a nutshell (may contain traces of being nuts)

My mum is a typical artist: lovely, creative, fuzzy and amazing, and she has always struggled for cash. She has created wall hangings and drawings, designs and calligraphy. When she was pregnant she drew a series of pregnant animals where you would see the baby inside. When she was pregnant with me, she drew the seal, and my sister inspired the pregnant horse. I haven't seen those drawings for almost twenty years – nobody really has. She made a children's book I absolutely loved but it never sold. She made Christmas cards – really lovely ones with expensive prints because my mum does quality. Boxes of quality that stacked up in our house. My mum is a wonderful artist and, just like many talented people out there, she has spent most of her life worrying about money and how to make ends meet.

My dad worked to build up his law firm and put in long hours and even weekends to make the practice work. He wasn't at home much when we were small, but he wanted to pay the mortgage and his business to succeed. My parents separated when I was five and my sister was three. It's one of those typical stories of growing apart, and the big difference that ran between them was the way they invested their time, attention and – surprise, surprise – money. I grew up thinking that you either have to work really hard doing serious stuff all day and make money or you have fun and lots of people you can talk to but no cash. I found myself wanting to be business-minded like my dad and fun-lovingly expressive like my mum. I wanted it all – you know the type. The last thing I was going to do was resign myself to the 'you can't have it all' mentality that my teachers and mundane 9 to 5ers tried to press upon me.

I started my first business venture at the tender age of seven by selling rose water. I squished rose petals and mixed them with water so that it smelled really nice. Then I filtered the rose squish out. Tadaa! I thought I had discovered the way to natural rose perfume... Unfortunately it went brown and lost its smell after five minutes. It didn't turn out to be a sustainable business model. My second venture proved more lasting: selling hair accessories age thirteen. I made and sold them at the local artists' market with my friend Alice, who later got them into some shops, too. I loved the creative part. I could even do the selling at the stand but to approach a shop left me with the shivers. I hated the thought of being rejected.

The Artrepreneur: Financial Success for Artistic Souls

Fast forward: As my pocket money was scarce, I couldn't afford the cinema or luxuries like chocolates or lush presents as some of my friends did. I worked for extra money and it had two important effects on me:

1) I was proud to earn my own money.
2) I felt I was poor so that I had to work where other kids could just have fun, but I dreamed of 'the good life'.

After finishing school, I created and performed solo shows for the corporate world singing known songs, parodies and my own songs all strung along by a storyline. When it came to getting my music out there, I had no time to waste. I asked for an investment from my dad so that I could make a record. He asked for a business plan to be delivered first. At that time I was way too artistic to write a business plan but in reality that was my way of avoiding the fact that the numbers simply didn't add up. Dad didn't invest; I sulked and then produced my album anyway. I did it on a shoestring. Over time I produced three albums by just getting on with it, getting cheap deals and hoping it would all work out one day – but did it make business sense? Absolutely not.

Luckily life and doing what you love is not all about making business sense. Sense is multidimensional. My album production made artistic, brand and craft-building sense. Had I been as clear about this back then, I could have saved myself the constantly nagging doubts and painful frustrations that accompanied my life for years.

Doubting my own abilities and reasons cost me a lot more than cash...

My secret wish was that one day my music prince would come and make it all right. That I could show them all that my money, time and suffering would pay off big time. Just you wait! And I did. Fast forward again. I smile, looking down at the clouds below me. To think that I make money travelling the world, having just spent a wonderful week at the Sheraton in Cairo sipping cocktails (all paid for) at the pool, singing, acting and dancing my way around the globe though being beautifully independent of men in suits – managers/label/industry – and remaining the Queen of my own destiny. How wonderful! I even performed my own show at the Edinburgh Festival with a £25,000 budget. For seven years this had been a big dream but in 2009 I made it happen. I raised the funds, got the team, wrote the show, and enjoyed my entourage of twenty-three. The whole experience was amazing. Then, even though I run my own coaching business, which means that if I don't work I don't make money, I took two months out in 2010 to travel in South America. Me, the previously ever-broke, super-skint budget queen of idiosyncratic self-expression.

It wasn't luck, the blessing, the salvation of being discovered, Prince Wealthy or any of the romantic ideas I had held before. I'm no better than anyone else. Trust me, I've got lots of stuff to deal with. I am great at doubting myself. Sure, I've had some achievements, such as record deals (Sony Music), TV appearances, personal relationships, and I've transformed many of my beliefs and issues around money. Then I think to myself – hmm, that's not that great, it's not like you had a chart success, own ten record labels and made a million in year two. Other people have – just look at Oprah, Beyoncé, Madonna – now that's successful.

So who am I to write about money?

These are the reasons I am writing The Artrepreneur:

a) To provide clarity and authentic insight into a way of living that works for Artistic Souls. For you and for me.
b) I want to empower you to let go of your stuff around money and move on to be the powerful creator you are meant to be. It's fun to do it with a friend, so I am here to be your friend on this journey! Would you like to play with me?
c) I have a personal passion for finding a way of 'having it all', creating a way that works for us Artistic Souls. I wrote this book to pave this way for you, too.

Paul McKenna wrote the book ***I Can Make You Rich*** and I bought it with its orange sticker of 'save £6 at Waterstones' – spot the irony. Saving £6 on an 'I can make you rich book' – priceless. When I took the book to the counter, the guy next to me sniggered, "Yes, that's the way to get rich – just write a book about how to get rich!" The hidden remark is, of course, "What does the author know? He's just using my desire to fulfil his own and therefore taking from me to enrich only himself".

I will always remember this 'joke' my dad told me: a man sees an ad in the paper "How do you make $100,000 in 10 days with no work? Send us $10 and find out." The man sends $10 to the address and receives a letter with the following instruction: set up an ad in the paper with the headline "How do you make $100,000 in 10 days with no work? Send us $10 and find out" then add your address. Best wishes!

When my dad told me this, I thought it was funny. But by now I've seen too many people actually do this and take advantage of our hopes and dreams in a way that adds nothing but only takes. It makes me furious. At seminars and on websites I've followed my dreams and desires only to end up out of pocket with a book that says things I already know or I've spent three days listening to advice that doesn't sit right with my values and need for integrity.

This has led me to become very suspicious over the years so I won't blame you if you are too. However, if you spend money on learning and you do learn, the money hasn't been spent but actually well invested. My intention is to add as much value as I possibly can. Not just to make the investment of your money worthwhile, I want to shower you with value!

There are different ways to read this book:

You can read it purely to entertain yourself and be curious about what it has to say. Maybe you have a specific question you want answered or a problem you want to solve. It can be a good idea to write the question out and then go back after you finish and see if the book did answer this for you. Feel free to drop me a line about it!

Or you may wish to be completely open and listen deeply. Simply allow yourself to receive, enjoy the shifts in your attitude towards money and see how much fun you can have whilst educating yourself.

However you choose to use it, enjoy the journey and have fun.

Table of Contents

1. the NATURE Of The Artistic Soul

I am not interested in money. I just want to be wonderful.

Marilyn Monroe

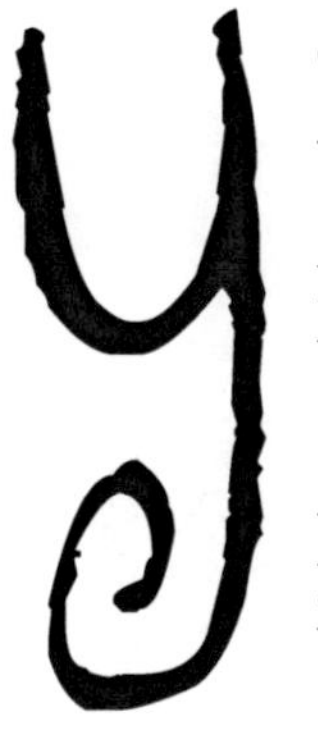

ou don't have to be an artist to be in touch with your Artistic Soul.

The Artistic Soul is the deeper part of us that yearns to create, to express, to live from purpose and use life as a canvas for our imagination.

The more deeply connected you are to your Artistic Soul, the more you may feel different about yourself in this material world. We know we are living in this world but aren't really of it.

Actually I believe that everyone is an artist at the core of their true being (but shhh, that's a secret).

I go as far as referring to the reader and myself as Artistic Souls because this book was written for people who identify with the sensitive, creative heart of all things.

There are plenty of books telling you how to make money or how to build a business but I have always found they miss the point for me: I don't *just* want to build a business and money won't motivate me for long.

Artistic Souls have a high sense of awareness and are sensitive to the energy around them. They tend to take things very personally. They are great at seeing life from new angles and have a deep desire to express themselves, though it doesn't have to just be through words. I forget the name of the wonderful dancer who was asked by a journalist what she wanted to communicate through her choreography and dance. She said, "Darling, if I could put it into words, would I need to dance?" Artistic Souls feel life and translate the force into their chosen medium: dance, song, music, sound, clay, colour, businesses, projects, charity, theatre, film, words. They are the kind of people who come up with new ideas (all the time). Sometimes they feel haunted by their creativity and there is more information and tips on how to deal with that in my audio course *The Curse of Creativity,* which you can download free from my website www.brinkcoaching.co.uk or from www.artrepreneurbook.com.

Artistic Souls feed on inspiration like flowers on water and sunlight. With their head full of ideas and visions, they can struggle with the day-to-day business of life. Often they don't even have an everyday life. The mundane just doesn't compare to the colourful reality conjured up in their beautiful minds! So bureaucracy, finances, paying bills on time – these are usually not the strong points. Which has some harsh consequences for them. As my dad used to say, "Those who don't know about money will end up losing theirs to someone who does".

There are so many things that Artistic Souls hate, but the most common seem to be having to 'sell yourself' to get your work recognised and being trapped in a soul-destroying situation where you don't feel you have the freedom to do what you want because you don't have the money to do it. There will be many other factors that can kick in, but what I want to do here for you is reinvent Artistic Souls, so that those limiting factors no longer apply.

2. The Artrepreneur

Being good in
business is the
most fascinating
kind of art.
Making money is
art and working
is art and good
business is the

best ART.

Andy Warhol

Being an ARTrepreneur is all about combining our two major desires into one snazzy skill set: making money from our creativity.

Being an Artrepreneur means realising that we can use our creativity not only to make art, but also to apply it to the canvas of our life. Creativity means using our capacity to have fun and develop the platform for our overall success, including wealth.

When I talk about art I am referring to all forms of expression through any chosen medium. Art refers to creating something out of nothing. You will hear me refer to music and theatre, painting, media and business. From a character to a story, colour combinations to sounds, ideas to concepts, inventions to experiences.

Becoming an Artrepreneur is developing the skills that allow you to create what you want in your life. Money is one part of what you want.

Being an Artrepreneur is combining business skills with artistic values. It means translating the language and values of creativity into the world of business in order to 'have it all'.

I see the process of becoming a successful Artrepreneur in two major parts:

1) Healing issues, confusions, doubts, bad experiences and negative references to money. In other words getting over the idea that money is anything but a symbol.
2) Mastering creating in a financial context.

This book focuses primarily (though not exclusively) on part 1. Without that foundation part 2 is a closed door.

We will talk about creating money, saving money and the difference between spending and investing, too. You will feel clearer and walk away with new skills. Of course, there will always be more to learn.

Let's take the first steps first.

Many people keep asking themselves why they are the way they are. Or why they just can't seem to do something.

The Why question allows us to find opinions and insight into the past and the complexity of human thinking, which makes for great evening conversation but poor daytime success.

The time to result ratio, however, is rather high. It seems to me that a lot of time gets invested analysing why you can't do this or why you're like this or that but that doesn't actually bring the desired change. My conclusion: with your permission, I won't be wasting any more time than necessary on anything that doesn't really move us forward.

I won't be spending too much time on Why questions but we'll be looking more for 'what do we want?' and 'how can we get it?'

> *Luke*: But tell me why I can't...
> *Yoda*: No, no! There is no "why".
> (*Star Wars*)

My goal is to make the world of money accessible to the creative-minded in a soulful, fun and easy way.

3. the borders
Of Your World

The only reason people get lost in thought is because it's UNFAMILIAR territory.

Paul Fix (Actor)

Have you ever felt you have come to the edge of your world? It's the place where whatever is happening doesn't compute with your own understanding of how the world works. Stephen R. Covey describes the way we see the world as 'paradigms'. Paradigms are our maps for reality. But as you know, the map is not the territory. So just because I know where Camden Town is on the map and can put my finger on it and imagine how punk music originated there, I haven't been there and experienced the vibrant colourful madness yet.

In our psychological make-up, we have internal representations of the world (paradigms). Our experience of what life is like is defined by those paradigms as we tend to follow our map rather closely. In other words, the world looks a certain way to you depending on your internal map of it. When I first heard this, I was quite perplexed. I used to think that my inner map was defined by the outer world. I grow up and have experiences and therefore create my map of how the world is. Experiences imprint onto our inner map and that is how we project what we expect onto the outer world.

Covey remarks that when you try to find your way in Chicago with a map of Detroit, you can try as hard as you like, and improve yourself as much as you like, it will still be hard to find your way because the map is inaccurate. If in my internal/ subconscious/(map of the) world 'rich people are criminals', I'll find it hard to trust anyone who is wealthy. If I think 'making money is hard for me,', chances are that, in my world, that's exactly how it is.

It is often only when we come to the borders of our world that we first realise there is an edge or barrier. We realise we're there when things just don't make sense. Imagine you're someone who thinks that it takes time to set up your business but it will happen eventually and success will come. Then someone starts a business and in six weeks has it up and running. That would disprove the whole truth of 'things take time and happen eventually' and present you with a new mindset (for example) that supports the phenomenon of 'I can do what I need to do right now and get things going now'. A different way of thinking that leads to different results.

Personal growth means to shift into new paradigms, new mindsets, that mean adapting the map to reality. That is, you need to get a map of Chicago to get around in Chicago and nurture supporting views that serve what you actually want to do.

I want to encourage you in this book to discover the borders of your world and to g(r)o(w) beyond them!

Let's celebrate each courageous step you are taking. My personal celebration sound is an exclaimed, woohoooo! It's easy to put yourself down and too often we forget to acknowledge when we do something new, something cool. We think, 'that's normal' and maybe, 'I should have done that a long time ago'. But when you see a toddler learning to walk, it's being met with applause and praise. Every time they fall down, we go, "Well done, get up and go again!" We don't say, "You're such a loser, you'll never get it, watch yourself falling down over and over again". And when the little one gets it, don't we all applaud and go all 'hoochie coochie'? Or, for the designer fans, Gucci, Gucci.

But as an adult, I've observed we often just say, "Yeah, so what? I did okay. There is a lot I haven't got right yet, I'd better get going. Let's not rest on our laurels here. It's about time I did this little step and besides that's not really enough to get me to xyz." Just what is it about xyz anyway? What is there at xyz? I can't locate that place anywhere – I want to go to xyz one day and find out if it's really as good as we think. So – when you reach a border of your world and you are exploring something new in this book, or even when you recognise a place you've been stuck in, please celebrate. I would. "I was stuck here, I can see it now. Haha, and I can shift from here, I can move, I am free to make new choices, especially now that I see more options. Well done me. Woohoooo!"

That's the monologue that is much more helpful and fun. Feel free to use my words or replace them with even more eloquent ones from your own superb creative vocabulary. As long as you add the woohoo, because that, I would say, is an essential part of the process. Shifting paradigms is all about growing. And that is beautiful and beauty is good. Growth is freedom and some – like Steve Chandler – would go as far as to say that growth is happiness. In fact, I'd like to say growth is an essential part of happiness.

Let's grow in our authentic financial fun consciousness!

In the past, when I met people who got rich doing what they loved, it blew my mind (what a great expression – bang!) In my world at that time you must have been incredibly lucky for that to happen, but then I'd hear that these people didn't consider themselves lucky. Which screamed of arrogance to me because, in my world, they HAD to be lucky for this to happen – how else could it be? I was at the border of my world. That's why to me, Anita Roddick, founder of the Body

Shop, was a superhero. She did what I would have deemed impossible: created and ran a positive business! She was someone I could accept being very successful because she had a great idea (sourcing natural ingredients all over the world and doing fair trade) and did lots of good in the world (setting up fair trade on cosmetic ingredients, no animal testing, modern branding and quality products). I loved that.

Anita Roddick obviously knew what she was doing. But how do you get to know what you are doing, especially when you are doing something that hasn't been done before? Let's find out.

How can you connect success and doing what you love?

That was me right at the edge... at the border of my world. The map I had just didn't have those territories marked on it! It was unexplored ground. The music business is a good example to understand the different nature and focus of using creativity. As a business, the orientation is money and a business only works when money is generated. But, for an artist, the primary orientation is creativity and expression. When these two orientations/worlds clash, our conflicts rise to the top and it's a question of time until our emotional volcano erupts. So what's the solution?

How can we have it all?

For a long time I thought having a record deal would be the solution to making money from music because, with business people behind the artist, the creative doesn't have to do the 'dirty work'. Well, not true because the artist becomes the 'product' that gets sold and has to sell themself and their 'brand'. Turning a free spirit into a brand can be very tricky, and this holds true in every industry.

> We can't solve problems by using the same kind of thinking we used when we created them.
>
> Albert Einstein

The way we see the problem IS the problem (says Covey and now I said it, quoting him!) The way we think about our world defines its borders and so the borders of our world limit us from going further. Often these borders are invisible/unconscious and we only see them from the other side. We can't get over the border of a world we thought up – just as we can't solve the problem with the thinking that created it. But just as with invisible ink, when you take a black light (which isn't really black) you can see the writing clearly. This book is a practical makeover of your money mindset. Just like in the good property programmes on television where they transform the simple flat into people's dream home, I want to transform your financial make-up into a wonderful landscape that allows you to freely create the life you really want to live.

Enjoy the expansion of your thinking as we shine the black light onto the invisible ink of those subconscious rules that have held you back before.

The way we think about our world defines its borders. We want to recognise and celebrate the borders of our world and g(r)o(w) beyond them.

You don't need to try harder doing what you've done before; you don't need to work endlessly on yourself to improve yourself in the hope of better results. You may just need a new and better map that describes the world you live in more accurately and that's easier to use. A new way of seeing that will allow you to create a very different experience.

Are you getting excited? Can I hear a wooohooo?

4. What is your Problem With Money?

I don't have a problem with money. I have a problem with NOT HAVING money.

Evelyne Brink

would love to say that I am free from any 'issues' when it comes to money because I've made following my heart my tour guide through life. "Do what you love and the money will follow!"

But I would be lying. Any of these ring true for you too?

- Do you wish you had it all but hate the idea of giving up what you love for it?
- Do you feel suspicious about people with money, wondering where they got it from and how many people they must have screwed over to get it?
- How jealous do you get when others get more, often for doing less than you do?

What I have often said is that I don't have a problem with money. I have a problem with not having money and, with the clarity of hindsight, the truth is that as much as I made my art and craft the main importance my life has been very much ruled by money: the lack thereof, the confusion and helplessness around it. We all have our story we tell ourselves and other people and often the money story is one of the most powerful tales we tell. Unfortunately power doesn't equate to 'good use of force'. We must learn to use the force as Yoda would remind us. Ten years ago, I found myself a true victim of my thoughts and feelings, especially when it came to feeling poor. Here's how it went:

> I can't afford anything! I am soo poor. How do you afford THAT? Like a hungry stray cat I'd sneak around the buffet at the gorgeous Sanctuary restaurant in Thailand.

(Notice I made it to Thailand – three months of hanging out! – and others asked me, "How can you afford THAT?")

I had to keep costs down, so I ate only the foods in the bottom third (price wise) of the menu. Thailand is cheap and even the most expensive meals would be far cheaper than at home but such was my (perceived) poverty that I would not allow myself to spend more than absolutely necessary.

The popular terminology that seemed to back up my tightness around spending was 'to be on a budget'. I like the idea of having a budget but I find it often to be a phrase used to disguise 'want to be as cheap as possible whatever that means because I don't know how to control my spending otherwise'. I'm on a budget sounded fancy and as though I was in control. Sure, I had a certain amount of money in my bank account but that doesn't define how much of it could be used for food or shelter – I didn't know what I would need so I just somehow would spend and hope for the best. I certainly wasn't as advanced as having **purposefully chosen budgets** or being able to stick to them if I'd had them!

I wrote down every single purchase I made in little journals and then did the maths (if I didn't forget in between) of how little I was spending. Every time I looked at it I would be reprimanding myself because, after all, it all adds up. "OMG, look how much you spent!" Trying to keep the costs as close to zero as possible, I was fighting a losing battle. I would say that my problem with money was that I didn't have enough. Most people I have met, coached, and talked to would blame the not having enough as the root cause of their money troubles.

If I had more, there would be no problem.

It reminds me of playing that game where you hold your hands in front of your eyes and assume that because you can't see others won't see you. I can't see you therefore you do not exist. I get the logic of it but it just doesn't hold to be true. When we're kids there is a time we think that's how it works. Then we realise it doesn't. It's the same here. The *feeling* is of not having enough money and, that being the problem, interestingly enough it does NOT necessarily disappear with more money. It just looks as if it does. Whatever money issues you have, you are likely to have them with increased numbers, too.

It's our relationship to money that will define our true wealth.

When we don't resolve a conflict, it tends to resurface and our conflicts with money are no different. Whatever the problem, what you resist persists. Wealth has less to do with the numbers in your bank account than you may think. Having money in the bank alone is not going to make you financially free. There are plenty of millionaires out there with huge money anxieties driven to prudent saving mentalities. The most generous people are often not the richest – as the *New York Times* reported in 2005.

> Working-age Americans who make $50,000 to $100,000 a year are two to six times more generous in the share of their investment assets that they give to charity than those Americans who make more than $10 million, a pioneering study of federal tax data shows.

But what's the point of having the money in the bank when you're living like someone who hasn't? What's rich about having money and not enjoying it? I would like to suggest that wealth is all-round abundance from having money in the bank to the options and possibilities you have and allow yourself to experience.

A useful definition of wealth needs to include the well-being you feel around money.

The wonderful news is that the better you feel around money, the easier it will be to create it.

An Inside-Out Approach

There are many ways to look at our problems. We want to be fun and effective and therefore I'd like to introduce you to the inside-out approach of being in the world. I'd like to differentiate between the Do-Have-Be model and the Be-Do-Have model.

The Do-Have-Be model suggests you must:

a) Do (work hard) in order to have (money).
b) Have in order to be (happy).

Here is a typical Do-Have-Bee in action:

But it's outdated and doesn't really work long term. Too many heart attacks stop the Do-Have-Bees from actually enjoying their life, leaving them with stress and compromise that is literally sickening.

The Be-Do-Have model – also known as the inside-out approach – suggests that Being and Having and Doing are independent of each other. Which isn't to say they don't influence each other; it's just that you don't need one to have the other. So you can start with Being or becoming happy, Do (what you love) and Have (what you want). Be-Do-Have people will swear that it's easier to get the stuff when you are already happy.

Finance is a loaded subject: many people would rather give intimate details of their sex life than let you in on their real financial situation. Money is intimate stuff, but actually it's not really money, it's the way we feel about it. It is all the hidden feelings, anxieties and darkness that can creep up when it comes down to cash.

The problem with money is not just that we do or don't have it. It's how we feel about having or not having it.

Our thoughts, or let's call it the mind, can be like a young dog around money. If you let the puppy run wild, it will take control of you. It will run around like crazy pulling you along on the lead and you will end up breathless running after it. Everything revolves around that dog and its fickle interests and excitements; there is hardly time for you to breathe – watch out, it went for the vase and is now running into the road again! But if we train the dog, it's man's best friend. When we train our mind around money, we become good friends. So much fun to play with! Salary: SIT! Good cashy, good cashy.

Artrepreneur Principle 3:

Money is man's best friend. But you've got to tame your thoughts around it.

5. the Money Story

I'm as poor as a
church mouse that's
just had an enormous
tax bill on the very
day his wife ran off
with another mouse,
taking

ALL the cheese.

Rowan Atkinson

Many people suffer from making their story about money part of their identity. They say "I am poor – I am not the money-type – I'm a struggling/starving artist – that's just who I am". Well, that is just a story and, like any good film, the script was written off-set. The actors act out a given script and we too tend to act out the script of our beliefs. We all have some script we are following, whether we have become aware of it or not. Our parents' stories, cultural myths, our history: they all combine so we live out our own stories and we accept them as true. It makes sense we do that, but it makes even more sense to reflect on it now that we're adults.

If you run your life based on a bad script, it's going to be hard to feel good about money. A money mindset makeover includes feeling good about money: having it, creating it, investing it, spending it. We want to be happy and skilled in all those areas and so we need a good script. A movie with a bad script just won't be a great movie. Just like the maps, our scripts are another way of describing the paradigms we operate in.

Are you willing to re-write your script?

When you tell a child a scary story, they will easily experience fear. When we tell ourselves frightening money stories, we can scare ourselves silly. Quite childish, isn't it? You are not your story. You are far more than a story. Money has got nothing to do with who you really are. Whether you've got lots or none it will not change your value as a human being. It won't make you a better person because you have more cash in the bank and it won't take away whatever emptiness, pain or questions about life you have.

Contrary to popular belief, money is not a healer of insecurities.

It can act as a patch and cover them only for a while. I know this from knowing wealthy people and also learning from those who regularly work with them. When it comes to people living their money stories, all extremes can be observed. Try these:

- People with fancy cars and houses working every hour there is to keep up with a lifestyle that they designed to mask the important unanswered questions in life. Riches can be a beautiful distraction from the deep stuff.
- People with no money living out the story and image of the 'I don't need money' philosophy to cover up their insecurities about growing up and taking responsibility for themselves and others.
- People with the 'I just don't have it' story playing the helpless victim gaining attention through empathy.

For some people 'having no money' is a fashion, a lifestyle of roughing it and living on a minimum budget. To be fair, it can be part of the adventurous challenge of backpacking for example, but some people take it to a whole new level and will live out the 'coolness' of being poor. They have their own fashion around not having much, their own hairstyles that identify them as not being part of the mainstream. They will claim they don't have much, don't need much and don't want much and that's what's cool. They stick to their own community of living cheaply and dream of being completely self-sufficient – showing the capitalist assholes where it's at.

Likewise there is a bit of a pseudo-romantic notion about the impoverished artist; it is bohemian and that's unconventional and artistic. You are purely devoted to your art and so denounce consumerism and money. If you choose voluntary poverty in order to simplify your life or attain higher spiritual goals or make a point in society, that's all completely fine with me. What we are talking about here is not what's right and wrong. It's about having options, about choosing.

Being an Artrepreneur is not about becoming a commercial addict. Quite the opposite is true: what we are talking about here is the freedom to choose what you love. I am looking for inspired living, for truth, for love and for conscious choice to have a free and loving relationship with money. That is spiritual, and fun, and most of all simple.

Conscious choice can sound a bit dry, as if there is a lot of serious thinking involved and we would have to stay away from the light-hearted 'screw it, let's do it!' attitude, the carefree fun Artistic Souls (and billionaire business adventurer Richard Branson) love so much. But no, we are looking for consciousness in the sense of flow, growth, happiness, deep peace and big smiles. We like making choices based on clarity, not dogmas. Are you with me? Woohooo!

In the Western world there is also a snobbishness about the divide between old and new money. If you are rich from inherited wealth or land, or simply the length of time your family has been rich, then that is commonly accepted and acknowledged as being rightfully rich. People who newly come to riches through industry, business and now celebrity or showbusiness are snubbed or criticised.

So what are your feelings about money? Are you in the 'business is dirty' league or are you comfortable around it? Are you happy to get involved with finance or does money represent all that's wrong with the world and you would rather keep away – only looking at the necessary evil when absolutely necessary? Chances are that you are having some trouble around money – why would you pick a book with this title otherwise? – and may be feeling at least a little depleted and challenged about the topic. However, as in every good movie, we shall discover that our greatest weakness holds the seeds to our greatest accomplishments.

Heroes are known as people who have overcome their greatest challenges and fears. You can be a money hero and inspiration – there are definitely vacancies available.

Our greatest weaknesses hold within them the seed of our greatest strength.

We want to see things as they really are, not clouded by stuff, but not rose tinted and brainwashed either. I have no interest in spinning your views into a surrealistic orbit. But imagine being clear about money and creating a healthy functional relationship with it and how free you will feel when you become independent of the confusion and pain surrounding your financial life.

So just to sum this up so far: many people have issues with money, regardless of how much they actually have in the bank or grew up with. There are rich kids who always feel poor or think they can't do the things they really want, other rich kids who don't know how to value money and who throw it away. For people with no money, the issue may be about how to get some, for those with some, it's all about getting more; for those with more it's about keeping up with the lifestyle. Even millionaires may have money issues, fearing to lose it all, so just because you have got cash doesn't mean you have freedom around money. Step one is to accept this reality.

Money and our issues around it are two separate things.

The point is that no matter how much actual money we have, what holds us back from creating more is our story around money, the way we give meaning to it. When we identify ourselves with it we really make a bad deal. No amount of money, gold or valuables can add up to the value of your life. The most precious medium of exchange we have is the one we were born with. It's our time.

6. YOUR MONEY

Hi-story

I finally know what distinguishes man from other beasts: financial WORRIES.

Jules Renard (Author)

t's hard to give up smoking if you don't even know smoking is an issue for you. For alcoholics to 'recover' takes the recognition and acknowledgement of the condition first.

Likewise it's hard to create a healthy and creative relationship with money if you haven't woken up to issues around your current relationship with it – and that you are in one. You don't have to spend the next five years talking about your childhood to find out what's going on for you, but a little look into your past won't hurt. Indisputably, our attitude towards money has mostly been shaped by our parents, and our environment, as we grew up.

Our problem with money is also influenced by our cultural background. Just as an example, in the Middle Ages money was deemed a dirty business in the Christian culture; hence the Jews were left to deal with money and the business around it. In the Jewish culture money is not seen as dirty or disreputable. In fact, it's part of the Jewish culture to look after your finances and focus on financial success as part of caring for your family. It's quite interesting to look at your own background and see what went on in your cultural history. No doubt you would have been passed on stories that reflected that culture's attitude to money in one way or another, BUT please note that your future success does NOT depend on your background. Regardless of where you came from, you are free to go your own way.

Sometimes realising that the beliefs we deem as given aren't really ours is enough to release them. Sometimes you may need to look a little deeper into the nature of your thoughts to find that actually no thought really belongs to us. They are, rather, interchangeable and the more we detach from taking them so seriously the better time we tend to have in life.

Our hi-story with money forms our current story about money. A story is not truth; it's what we tell about the truth. To move from story to reality, it's good to know one from the other.

You have your money story and your money history. Both are only stories. One current. One past.

Before going all Zen on you, I have prepared a little quiz designed to explore the formation of your current relationship with money. Enjoy it, take it easy and have some fun with opening up the Pandora's box of your own past.

We have prepared a worksheet for you to go with the book. You can access your worksheet through the website www.artrepreneurbook.com

1) What was your father's relation to money? What did money mean to him?

____

____

____

2) Was your father's background abundant or scarce?

3) What was your mother's relation to money? What did it mean to her?

4) Was your mother's financial background abundant or scarce?

5) What did your dad tell you about money?

6) What is your culture's attitude to money? Is it clean? Dirty? Good to have? Important? Not to be worshipped?

7) What did your mother tell you about money?

8) What did your parents model to you around money?

____

____

____

9) How rich/poor did you feel growing up? On a scale with 10 being super-rich to 1 being super-poor?

____

____

____

10) How/where/when did you learn to make money?

____

____

____

11) What was your idea about getting rich?

____

____

____

This exercise is geared to create awareness and insight, but knowing about stuff and talking about it is great but it doesn't solve everything. We have to actually DO things differently if we want to produce different results. You will learn exactly what this 'differently' means and how to do those different things with creativity and gusto. So let's move further on!

7. What is Money? Part 1

What's Money?

A man is a success if he gets up in the morning and goes to bed at night and in between does what he wants to do.

Bob Dylan

ow, let's look at how **you** relate to money and what exactly money means to you. Here is another self-test. I still remember doing those Psychology tests in magazines and, yes, most of them were quite superficial and ended up telling me what type of person I apparently am. Well, this test is designed to help you discover for yourself what your relationship to money is. All you need to do is continue the following statements:

For example:

1) Money is...
   - A necessary evil
   - What everyone wants and only some get
   - Easy to make
   - Energy that flows
   - The excuse people use to not do what they want
   - Bad
   - Disgusting
   - Not important

   Your turn!
   (If you prefer to keep your book neat and fill out the exercise, download your worksheet at www.artrepreneurbook.com)

Money is:

___

___

___

People with money are:

___

___

___

Not having money means:

___

___

___

Making money implies:

___

___

___

What I would give to have money:

___

___

___

The answers to these questions will change depending on your mood and how you feel you are doing in life. For instance, if I took you to Venice with your loved one and asked you the same questions after you had the time of your life and a romantic meal at sunset, I'd get different answers than if asking you after your boss told you you're not performing to company standards, right?

Whatever your answers, they are your answers for now, and they will be great to work with, but they are not written in stone. Feel free to go through these questions as often as you like to explore how your opinions may be changing. As an inherently artistic creature I wouldn't be surprised if you had a great dynamic range of emotions, so explore them and enjoy yourself. To show you that you are not alone in this, I'll give you an insight into my own dark pits of money beliefs. This is what I think when I am down:

1) People with money are dodgy b****rds.
2) Not having money means being poor and struggling.
3) Making money implies doing the things I hate, and selling myself and my valuable time, in order to get things – basically to sacrifice what I love.
4) Answering the question what I would give to have money – it's already too much to ask. Money should be there for me and give to me! (give me what??) But I would consider giving my passion and skills to the world and accept money in return.

Are you inspired yet? You can see why I would have found it hard to make a lot of money. To me being honest and serving my soul will always rule over money – at least in the sense that I describe money here. What if money wasn't that icky thing of necessity but much more closely linked to our precious energy and divinity? Here are some suggestions from a more insightful place:

1) People with money are people. They have their happy days and their sad days and we all share the same desires and deep wish for happiness.
2) Not having money means it's time to play and create! Isn't it nice to get such an open invitation to grow and reap the benefits? Breakthroughs are amazing and make great inspirational stories as well!

3) Making money implies: doing what I love, personal growth, focus, making new friends and helping others have a better day/life.
4) What would I give to have money? I would give my best because I love giving. Money is a natural expression of my creativity and therefore the natural outcome of my efforts to love and share.

Who do you think has a more successful and fun day creating funds: the positive or negative Eve? So how do we switch? I hear you ask – well, I am assuming rather than actually hearing it. The answer is: through knowledge, insight, and understanding. I used to get so upset when I didn't understand maths at school for example but when it clicked all my anger disappeared and I started having fun – well, almost! I can get really angry in my relationship until I understand why on earth he did what in my world looked ignorant and selfish. As soon as I get it, my anger vanishes into the pleasant feeling of 'ahaa, aaah yeah'. Which is a sound effect shortcut for, 'I do understand now and feel peaceful with myself, musing at the realisation that you didn't mean harm but simply acted out of your own logical continuation of thoughts'.

Isn't it always like that? So let's get a deeper understanding and some ahaa, aaah yeah in relation to the ka-ching moment (please insert your own preferred sound effects).

8. What is Money

Part 2

Money is power, freedom, a cushion, the root of all evil, the sum of

blessings.

Carl Sandburg

Money is an exchange for value. You give me a painting and I give you money (in an ideal case scenario) or you give me food and I give you money. But the money is just a piece of paper, and the paper doesn't actually have that much value if you think about it. Producing a £20 note costs a fraction of what it represents. Which leads us a step further down the rabbit hole towards understanding your money mindset.

Money is only a symbol for value exchange and it all started at the marketplace long ago. If I trade a pig against a cow and need some bread, it's kind of hard to count the bread I get for my cow (though I am sure people would have done it) and it is heavy to carry a cow around in exchange for stuff, not even knowing if someone else would want my cow. So people started trading gold as the first agreed valuable exchange metal. Gold is only so valuable because there is a limited amount of it and we all agreed to use this as the basis of exchange. If suddenly people from another planet walked in, they might think gold is useless so it wouldn't be valuable to them. And if they didn't like gold because where they come from they feed their pigs with it, they wouldn't have the same appreciation for it.

When gold became the value-measuring metal, people started saving up their gold in vaults. Actually from what I've learned it was the goldsmith who made the coins who came up with the idea of offering safe space to keep your gold. He rented that out and would give people a 'note' that marked how much they had in the treasury. Soon people started trading the notes against goods as if they were the gold itself. And that's how money was born. So money is an IOU, a representation of something I have that I could give you (gold). Well, that's how it started, but then the goldsmith realised that people wouldn't all come back at once to get their gold so he started lending it to people who needed it and charged them a percentage of interest. So people got a notice that said "you have xx amount" and they paid that back with interest. But they never got the gold itself, just the note, and so the goldsmith was growing a neat business until people became suspicious about why he was getting so rich.

They thought he was spending their gold. Can you imagine the uproar? Scandalous! So they demanded to be shown to their vaults and 'tadaaaa!' all the gold was still there.

So they let him get on with business and you can see more on that in the little film *Money as Debt* by Paul Grignon, which explains the history of our money system. You will need forty-seven minutes to watch it, five minutes to make a cuppa, and it will change your view on things forever.

Here is the link: www.youtube.com/watch?v=vVkFb26u9g8

But why bother? Why do we need to know about this?

For us to be truly financially free, we want to liberate ourselves from our emotional attachment to money.

Understanding where it comes from, and what it is, will help you see the world much more clearly. Many of us grow up to believe that money is the thing we don't have enough of, the stuff everyone wants, what you mustn't spend too much of. Quite frankly that is one of the most limiting beliefs around! It's simply not true. Money is but a promise, so why would you want to get so stressed out about a promise? You can make a promise, right? Okay, then you can make money.

Can you keep your promises? If not, would you be willing to improve on that? I would like to suggest that keeping your promise is crucial. This idea may sound super-simple and that's why it is sooo powerful. Money itself is the promise that you should get the value of the number. And we just swap promises these days. Isn't that weird? We make the paper (on which the promise is written) mean so much! The wonderful thing about this system is that you take a promise paper and change it for an mp3 player or a computer or a banana.

We live in such a great world. Seriously, isn't it much smoother to exchange promise papers than stones or giraffes? Just in case you think trading a giraffe does sound good – it would also mean we'd come up against serious animal rights issues. Just imagine walking through Camden Town in London with a giraffe – okay, that actually does sound quite cool. However, it is just not feasible. Even if we didn't care about animal rights, or good living conditions for giraffes, what would the ticket fare for the underground be and would you be charged extra for the neck?

Let's stick to our promises. I just want to say this again: if you know how to make a promise and keep it, you can make money. More details to follow. This isn't the end of it – this is the beginning and it's important. Because often we make things so complicated it hurts. My dad once said to me, "Masters are those who can make complex issues look easy and explain them to a five-year-old. Fools are those who take simple things and make them complicated". Shame you never listen to your dad when you are young. On the note of not wanting to listen to your parents: Gregory Baton said, "Maturity is willingness to do what you want, even if your parents wanted that, too". Creative souls love straying from the subject so let's get back to the original point:

**Money doesn't make the world go around.
Giraffes don't either.**

Yes, they say it does (money, that is, not giraffes) because people are willing to move mountains for money and sometimes they mean it literally as in, you give me cash, I buy the dynamite and blow the *insert your favourite swear word in order to emphasise here* mountain up! If I have money, someone will do what I want in order to get it. Money is the determining factor. 'It's all about the money. Money is power.' But is it really?

Think about this: it's paper, or nowadays a number on a computer or statement if we're lucky. It can't do anything! Because it's only a promise and a promise itself doesn't change stuff. Carrying out the promise does. It's the people who carry out the promise that make the world go around. If I blow up the mountain, I blew up the mountain. Not the money. I think this is really important because it shifts the power back to the people. To YOU and me, baby.

Money doesn't have power. You have power.

We are the ones making it happen. Especially creative people because it takes creativity to come up with good ideas. It is people who make great things happen. People even make money. You are a person so you can make great things happen. You can make money.

9. So What Is The Real Problem With Money?

So you think that money is the root of all evil. Have you ever asked what is the

ROOT OF ALL

money?

Ayn Rand

he problem we have with money is that most of us are very confused around the topic. We grow up thinking that money makes the world go around. That money is power. That money is motivation. That money is the answer – and then we get very upset if we don't have it. As George Bernard Shaw said, "Money isn't the root of all evil. The lack of money is."

Money is a trading tool.

A hammer is a tool. You wouldn't get upset or too stressed about a hammer, would you? If you do, wow, you've got issues! My favourite story about the hammer is from Paul Watzlawick[1]:

> A man wants to hang a painting. He has the nail, but not the hammer. Therefore it occurs to him to go over to the neighbour and ask him to lend him his hammer. At this point, doubt sets in. "What if he doesn't want to lend me the hammer? Yesterday he barely spoke to me. Maybe he was in a hurry. Or, perhaps, he holds something against me. But why? I didn't do anything to him. If he would ask me to lend him something, I would, at once. How

---

1 "The situation is hopeless, but not serious", from *The Pursuit of Unhappiness* by Paul Watzlawick.

can he refuse to lend me his hammer? People like him make other people's life miserable. He will think that I need him because he has a hammer. No way!" He runs to the neighbour's door, rings, the neighbour opens but before he gets to say hello, the man screams, "You can keep your hammer, you bastard!"

I love this story because it illustrates so well how we dwell on stuff in our minds, making mountains out of molehills, convincing ourselves about how the world is and acting upon that. If you didn't have a hammer and needed one, would you be okay to ask for one? Or would you feel you needed to sell your soul to get it?

For most of us, if you really wanted a hammer, would you think about what to do with your life before getting one? Would you refuse every opportunity to get one because it's not completely in line with your ideas about how your life should be? If we replace the word 'hammer' with 'money' and fit it into common sentences such as "I want to make money from my paintings and I don't want to do anything else ...." then it starts sounding reasonably ridiculous: "I want to make hammers from my paintings, I don't want to do anything else to get a hammer – I have to make more hammers from acting – I love acting but they don't give me a lot of hammers for it."

If you for some reason struggled using the hammer, you'd go and get help, right? You'd ask if someone can show you how to use the thing. Okay, maybe you have other people do the hammering for you and at some point you'd get up and find out how to use it yourself. But you wouldn't cry over it. Unless you didn't ask before you hit your own finger – yes, that does hurt and it might well cause some tears. The point is you'd easily ask for help without necessarily feeling like a complete loser in life. You wouldn't beat yourself up about it, so why is it that we make such a big deal out of money? Because we make it mean more than it is: because we see the connection between the tool and the result of using the tool and confuse one with the other.

We think money means happiness, safety, well-being, acknowledgement, health, status, freedom, doing what you want. It's like saying the hammer makes me comfortable and happy. Hammers are freedom. Hammers are security. I can only be happy when I have enough hammers. By the way, if the hammer doesn't do it for you, use giraffes. So here is the big secret of being an Artrepreneur – let's hammer it in:

Money does not mean anything unless you make it mean something.

So stop being unkind about it, cut yourself some slack. There is no real need to make money mean anything fundamental. You are a wonderful, worthy, beautiful human being no matter how many or how few hammers you make or have. It doesn't matter how big or small your hammer is either

– that almost sounds a bit naughty, that bit about the size of your hammer, but you know what I'm saying.

Your personal value does not depend on that. If you are a dog, playing fetch may be fun. Michael Neill introduced me to the idea that we play fetch with our goals. I'd like to add we play fetch with our desire for money. You tie your well-being and feeling of safety and happiness around the bone and throw it as far away as you possibly can and then you run after it like a good dog. When you get it, when you achieve your goal, you wag your tail. Good doggy, happy doggy. That sensation lasts for a little while, but it wears off and then you want another hit of good feeling. So you throw the bone again and with it goes your well-being and happiness. You start running again and, more often than not, the bone lands in the bushes and you have a pretty adventurous hunt ahead. Trying to find your happiness somewhere, out there.

We tie our well-being, our happiness, around the financial bone and try to get it. We throw the bone by setting higher and higher financial goals and expectations. "I need a house. I have a family to feed. I need a new car. I want a high definition super whatever TV" – and then we run and try to fetch the bone. And we get it and we can gnaw on it for a while and then we throw it again. When we don't get it fast enough, we get really upset and ask, "Will I ever be happy?" Fetch is a fun game if you are a dog. Now some would say that life is a bitch...

So let's stop making money more than it is and start recognising it for its real value. Money is crucial to create in our world. I grew up with plenty of anxiety around the topic. My whole thing was, "I don't have enough money to do what I really want". My big fear was that I may have to end up doing what I hated because of money. I see people all around me do just that. "I don't like my job but I have to pay the bills," they say, completely ignoring the idea that there are jobs you may like that also pay the bills. "Yeah, but you gotta be lucky to get those," they would probably say. "There are not enough for everyone." Ask Richard Branson, founder of the Virgin group (Virgin records, Virgin airlines, Virgin gyms etc) and he will not say that luck made him. In fact, no successful business person will!

We might not know this, we might still believe in being lucky – after all, that's what those who don't know call the 'magic' – so then we make up our own part of the story. "I hope I'll be lucky." Some of us are very positive and tell ourselves that it will all work out. I was a bit like that and I was also a bit like the people who are always afraid that it won't. Which makes for ongoing passionate discussions with myself in my head. Well, at least I kept myself entertained or whatever it's called when you're too wrapped up in your own world to enjoy the real action.

Then I learned about the importance of controlling your mind, which made for a big challenge as my thoughts were running amok on a daily basis. But I was taught that your thoughts create your reality, so now I got paranoid that all my fears would come true. AAAAAaargh. I learned that you must not dwell in negativity because that only creates more negativity. So when negative thoughts came up – and they did come up a lot especially around money – then I didn't know what to do. Consequently, I told myself that it was really no wonder success wasn't working out for me if I was thinking like this! As long as we think inside the problem, we can't really expect a solution. That's what my dear friend with the great hair, Albert Einstein, explains so well: "We cannot solve problems with the thinking that created them" (and I'll quote him again and again because it's so true).

Why am I telling you all about my past thinking? Because I want to share that no matter how you are thinking now, you can change your thoughts and change your life. Or, more precisely, when you learn about the nature of your mind and thinking itself, things become much easier. The problem with money is defined by whatever we think about it and how we react to these thoughts, how deeply we buy into the thoughts themselves. Thinking can be changed. Life can be transformed. Because we have a wonderful gift called consciousness and making choices – otherwise known as growing up.

10. the Cinderella Syndrome

The idea of my
life as a fairy
tale is itself a

fairy tale.

Grace Kelly

Waiting for things to happen for you is like waiting for your Prince to come. The idea that one day someone will come to 'make it all good', the Cinderella Syndrome, applies to all genders, not only women get stuck in it. The Cinderella Syndrome has us in the waiting position... waiting... waiting. Not doing much. Living the vida pasiva (instead of the samba style vida loca as introduced by singer Ricky Martin). It's draining. It's boring, you'll catch yourself snoring, and not much happens. Your personal power goes down and it all feels like, 'Oh well, I guess that's just how it is' and you send lots of text messages with 'LOL' (for those to whom LOL still means 'laughing out loud' and not just 'lots of love') and smiley faces whilst your own face doesn't really move much.

I can spot people stuck in the Cinderella mode from miles away because I spent so much time waiting for my own salvation. Living in the imagined future of 'when I'm famous, then all will be well' or in the fantasy of 'when I am married and have children all will be well', I developed the habit of expecting the future to solve the issues of the present. There are two problems with this model. They become apparent:

1) When the Prince doesn't come – most common.
2) When the Prince cometh – which as you will see may turn out to be even worse!

If you are living the Cinderella Syndrome, you are the damsel in distress waiting to be saved by the Prince who will make it all right – you are in for a long wait. I don't know about you but I hate waiting. When is life finally happening?

When are things finally going to be well? Will we ever know? To make the wait sweeter, why not engage in time-passing activities such as watching daytime TV or crossword puzzles? Here is one I made earlier:

Start writing to fill in the numbered field:

Time Sweetening Crossword Puzzle

1↓: Question word about an object.
2↓: Opposite of off.
3→: Our planet.
4↓: Conjugation of 'to be' second person singular.
5→: What you say to a person talked to directly in three letters.
6→: The equivalent of taking action.

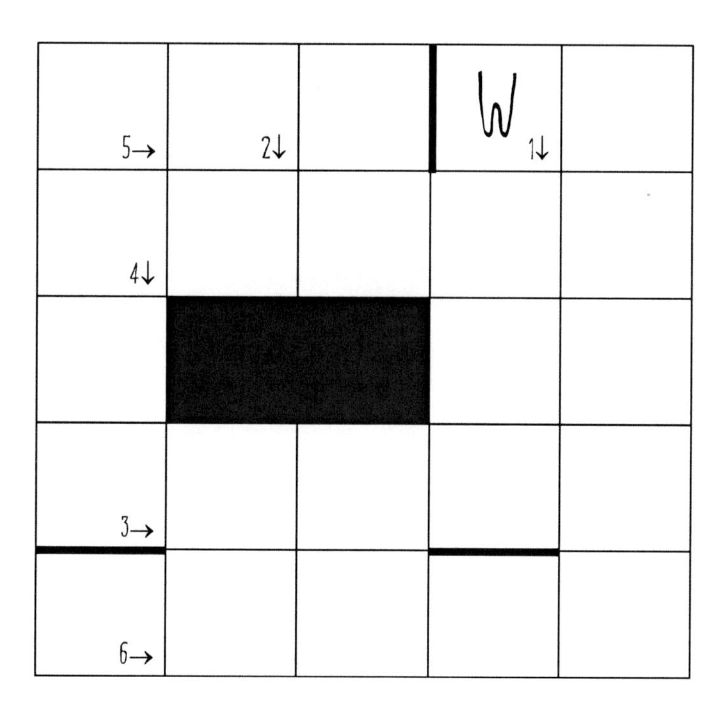

Now string words 1–6 together for your winning sentence. Are we having fun yet? (If you have difficulty with this, turn to the Resources section.)

If the Prince doesn't come, you just spent what is known as 'the best years of your life' waiting. Wow. That's a great story to inspire your grandchildren with. Oh, and apart from inspiring the grandchildren – what about yourself? Now? Yeah, you could be living inspired NOW!

If the Prince cometh, it's hard because the fantasy may be lived out but the satisfaction still won't be there. The truth is nobody can make it good for you. Over time, short term, you may fool yourself into believing and feeling they can but after a while even the greatest love chemistry will change. You get used to the greatest gifts. You will even get used to having money in your life. As humans, we simply adapt to our situation and this is called the principle of hedonic adaptation[2]. So even if 'the situation' improves through Mr or Ms Prince/ the Lottery/Financial Showers, you will adapt to it and the satisfaction vanishes with a 'poof'. That's a sound effect, in case you wondered, and not a gay fairy.

The 'pooff' doesn't always happen in an audible fashion but you will notice when your satisfaction is gone.

Have you noticed that fairy tales always end at the wedding and then they say "and they lived happily ever after"? That's code language for 'and that's where the trouble started but we don't want to go there, really'. If we told you Cinderella felt patronised by the Prince only two years later and didn't like the way the castle was cleaned and how her friends the mice and the birds were poisoned because they were seen as pests not as pets, boy – we'd be in for something. Imagine the arguments! And do they even have a social life? What if the Prince isn't as good a lover as we'd expect him to be? Maybe his hammer is a little too small. Or Cinderella likes girls after all?

Or in the more conventional scenario – she'd find that she always was under the care and command of someone else, first at home, now at the castle. She really hasn't found what she likes and she falls into a deep melancholy. It feels just like a hundred year sleep, but no kiss can wake her this time... or can it? Is fate that cruel... new Prince, new luck? Humans

---

2 Shane Frederick and George Loewenstein (1999) "Hedonic Adaptation" in Daniel Kahneman, Ed Diener and Norbert Schwarz (eds), *Scientific Perspectives on Enjoyment, Suffering and Well-Being*. Sonja Lyubormirsky, (2010) *The How of Happiness*, p.47 "The curious and powerful phenomenon of hedonic adaptation".

tend to find it really challenging to deal with having what they want. Or in other words: life goes on.

We think it would solve our problems; find out it doesn't and get really confused at the best of times, heavily depressed and aggressive at the worst. I want to adapt this: humans often find it challenging to deal with having what they **thought** they wanted. Being stuck in Cinderella mode is living life as a dream. But it's not a good dream.

There is a clear distinction between living out your dream and living in a dream.

Creating your dreams is powerful. Living in a dream is powerless.

By the way, what's the story with the glass slipper? Don't we wear shoes to protect our feet from stepping into glass? To wear a shoe made from that very material is rather counterproductive and, apart from that, very uncomfortable. I'm sure the chiropodist would agree that it would cause joint pain, back and knee issues, is very impractical and the sweat can't go anywhere in glass. It would be all over the tabloids: Cinderella got prince and smelly feet – Joint fears over new royalty.

Cinderella is not a good dream. Time to wake up. The most powerful awakening is the awakening to your own power – to being the creator of your life. As Steve Chandler says, becoming an "owner" or, in Stephen Covey's words, becoming 'proactive'. As an owner or creator you commit, you make things happen. You stop making the how a reason to stop you and focus on the what. So, Cinderella, stop waiting for the Prince (or Princess or Lady Prince or Prince dressed in Ladies' clothes – gosh, these days you've got to cater for everything). You are a Princess waiting to happen (well, some of you) and the only one who can make that happen is you. For our male readers – you are a bad-ass Prince. Now kick some butt.

11. CONSCIOUS

Money Making

A wise man
should have
money in his
head, but not in
his heart

Jonathan Swift

Brian Whetten PhD., M.A. is a personal and business coach who introduced me to some very useful imagery to understand why making money and business can be so hard for those with a consciousness geared towards joy, creativity and love. He explained how we can move beyond that – in fact, he did it so well I hired him as my personal coach.

First, imagine your experiences of life are defined by a ladder of consciousness. At the top of the ladder are the experiences we want such as love, joy, inspiration, creativity and deep happiness.

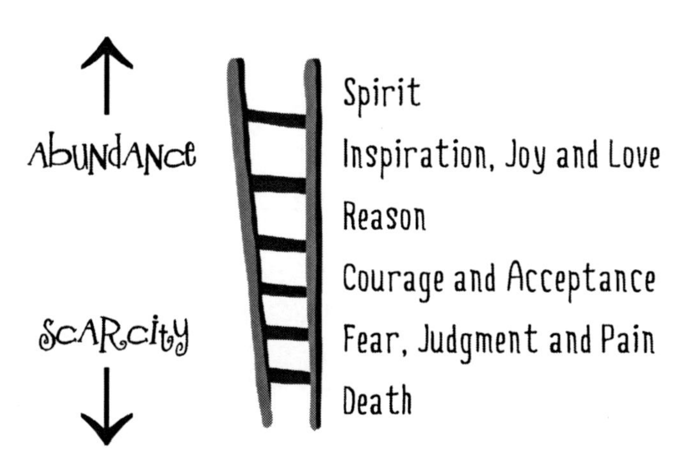

At the bottom of the ladder we find what we least want: death, fear, guilt, anger and shame. Business, as it is most commonly practised, operates from the lower part of the ladder. It's often based on fear, lack, scarcity and the assumption that there aren't enough resources.

That is the 'Hurry, only five left! Act now to avoid disappointment' mindset that has you reaching for your credit card. Our capitalist society is based on economic principles such as the law of supply and demand. When there isn't enough and many people want it, we can raise the price (e.g. housing in any major city) and when there is more than people need or want, prices go down (e.g. electronics). The underlying principle of this is scarcity and the idea that resources are limited. In housing this means a limited supply and inability to build more due to non-availability of suitable land and town planning regulations.

To oppose this, there are also spiritual laws, such as the law of abundance, which refers to the idea that there is more than enough and we can all enjoy it. I love how we are coming to use limitless resources now such as wind energy, sun energy rather than limited resources such as oil and gas. Oil runs out, wind won't. The Internet and its limitless capacity is also a great demonstration of this principle. Looking out from the top of the ladder we live life from abundance; there is more than enough and we live by the insight that our greatest joy doesn't come from taking but from giving. That giving produces more joy than taking has been proven in scientific studies by Positive Psychologists such as Dr Martin Seligman[3].

As we want to live at the top of the ladder of consciousness, living from joy and abundance, we want to do good in the world so we will also feel a big gap between

---

3 The fast growing field of happiness research is based on Martin Seligman's foundation of 'positive psychology' in the year 2000. (Marci Shimoff's *Happy For No Reason* and *Love For No Reason* will give you more insight into those studies as will Martin Seligman's *Learned Optimism*.)

offering our service or art and selling it. However, money making as we know it is more often practised from the bottom part of the ladder. The more conscious you are, the bigger that gap.

This is a biggie for most Artistic Souls. You're great at what you do and hugely passionate but you hate selling it. Selling means everything between the sale of a picture, client acquisition, getting an agent and whatever else it translates to in your field. You hate it because the selling aspect doesn't resonate with your generous nature of being loving and fun and giving, at least not when 'selling' is based on 'taking something'. And let's face it – the way we've come to know selling is by being sold at by advertisements, internet marketing, media and telephone salespeople interrupting our dinner. They want our money and demand our attention so it's easy to understand if you don't want anything to do with it.

There are essentially only three options to dealing with the conflict, as Brian Whetten points out:

1) You refuse to compromise your values and do the 'poor but pure' approach.
2) You compromise your values out of necessity.
3) You procrastinate the selling/moneymaking/business part.

I personally refused to go into anything that would compromise my values. I did the 'poor but pure' thing. I wasn't going to sell out under any circumstances. Never! What we want to do here is to create a new paradigm for selling which allows us to connect the top of the ladder with the bottom or, as Brian would say "create a conscious marriage of the two". Well, by now we've had some extensive flirting with the idea of happy money making – you've even started dating (by reading this book) – let's move on together and really get engaged in the material.

Let's take it one happy step at a time.

12. the Reason why

When I chased after money, I never had enough. When I got my life on purpose and focused on giving of myself and everything that arrived into my life, then I was

PROSPEROUS.

Dr Wayne Dyer

Making money and being conscious and giving – doesn't that all sound nice? One thing that differentiates a good book from real life is that the content and its grand ideas are in the book, and it works well in the examples, but then there is life and that's still separate from the book. So let's get practical again and connect what is offered here to YOUR life.

Business or Art?

A lot of great art has actually been created out of financial necessity. For example, Mozart's opera *The Magic Flute* was quite a commercial venture. It was written rather quickly, he was paid a lot, made it colourful, light-hearted and easily digestible for the masses.

It is still in the top ten of the most popular operas and frequently performed. It is also a timelessly beautiful work of – well – art! Historically, most classical musicians were ordered to compose in a certain style for their patron, the King or Pope or whichever aristocrat employed them. It was in their spare time that they created and explored new areas of musical development. Painters were hired to produce the royal portraits and that's how they'd make their living. It gave them the money that allowed them to explore their artistic development.

Michelangelo was a highly commercial artist – in fact, as he got more popular, he'd have the work done by unknown artists and merely add some finishing touches and his signature. He had students who did more of the work than he did, and he had a real business going. If he had to create each 'Michelangelo' from start to finish, he wouldn't have been able to be quite as prolific. His work became a brand. The same principle applies in film music: Hans Zimmer, who has composed many of Hollywood's classics, also won't be found writing every score note by note but has a team of high-level but less famous composers behind him who do the legwork.

Walt Disney movies aren't all drawn by good ol' Walt – he's got a team of artists who know the style and get on with the work. Not only do they know the style, they've even changed medium from hand drawing to computer animation and we still recognise a 'real Disney'.

Art can be generated in a variety of ways – it's not all bad or all good. For the purpose of our makeover, we want to learn to drop the judgement. It is whatever it is. However, having a good reason why we want to create money in our lives generates the right energy. When my reason was 'to finally stop moaning about not having enough money' my motivation was short-lived. I would take some actions, see results and stop moaning. Then as the goal was achieved I'd stop the actions and would be out of cash pretty quickly, only to start the cycle of moaning again. Boohoo.

We need a really good reason to actually WANT money. When I say a good reason, how about a hundred?

Exercise:
This was presented to me first by Michael Neill and starts juicing up your brain muscles to think in different terms. Write out a hundred reasons why you want to create money in your life. Write down the obvious, and not so obvious. Be open to discoveries. You can download your worksheet for this from www.artrepreneurbook.com

My hundred reasons to make money are:

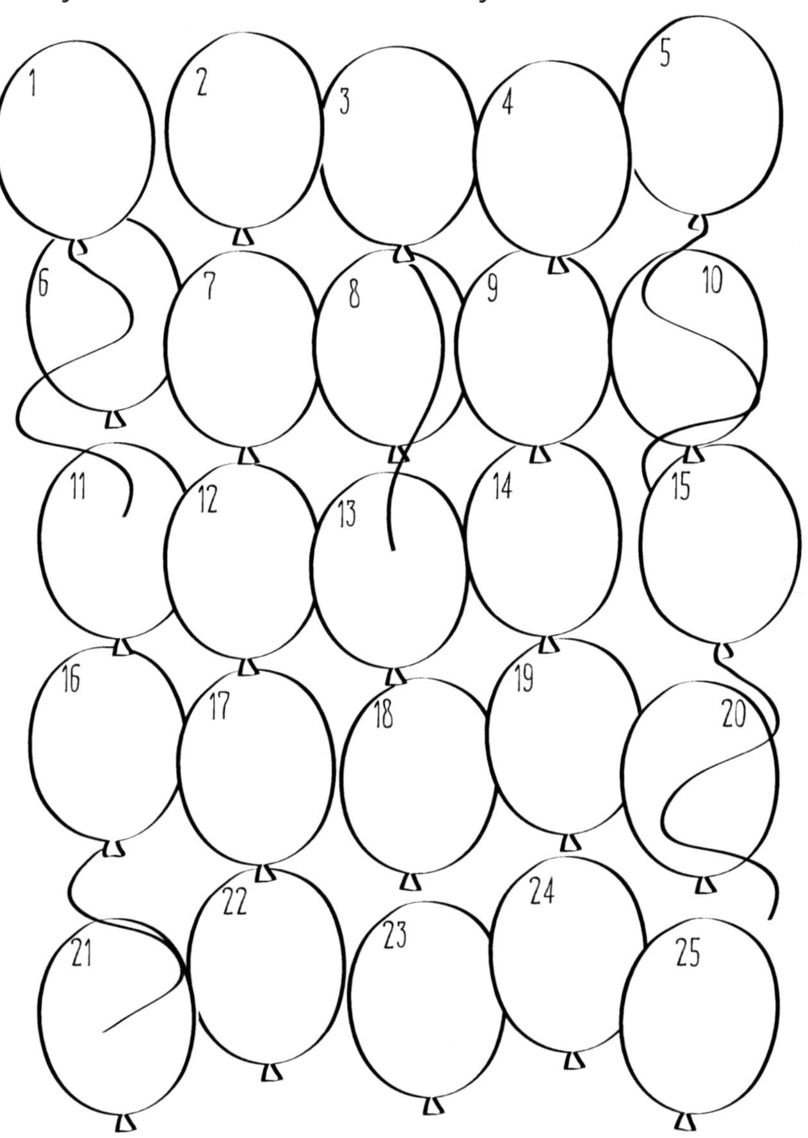

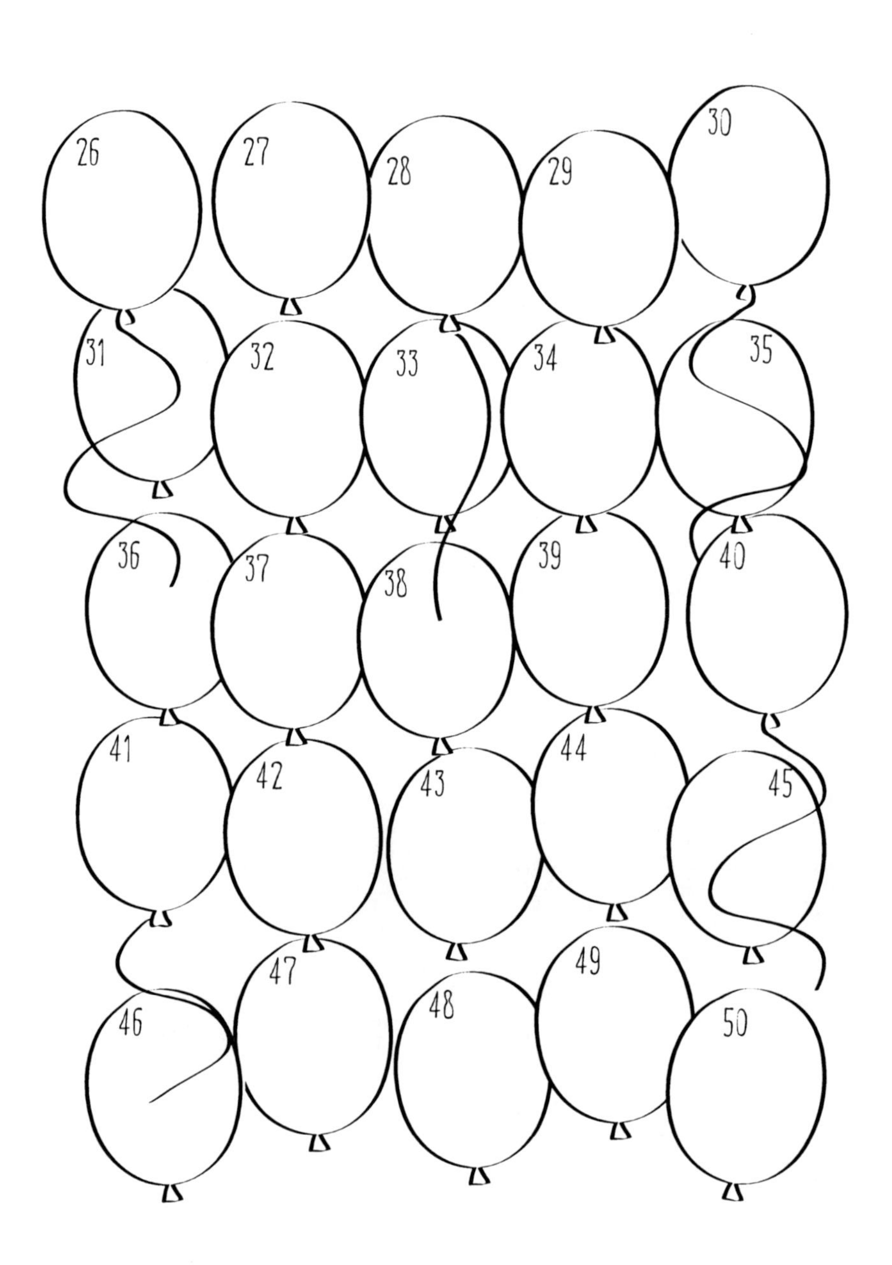
26
27
28
29
30
31
32
33
34
35
36
37
38
39
40
41
42
43
44
45
46
47
48
49
50

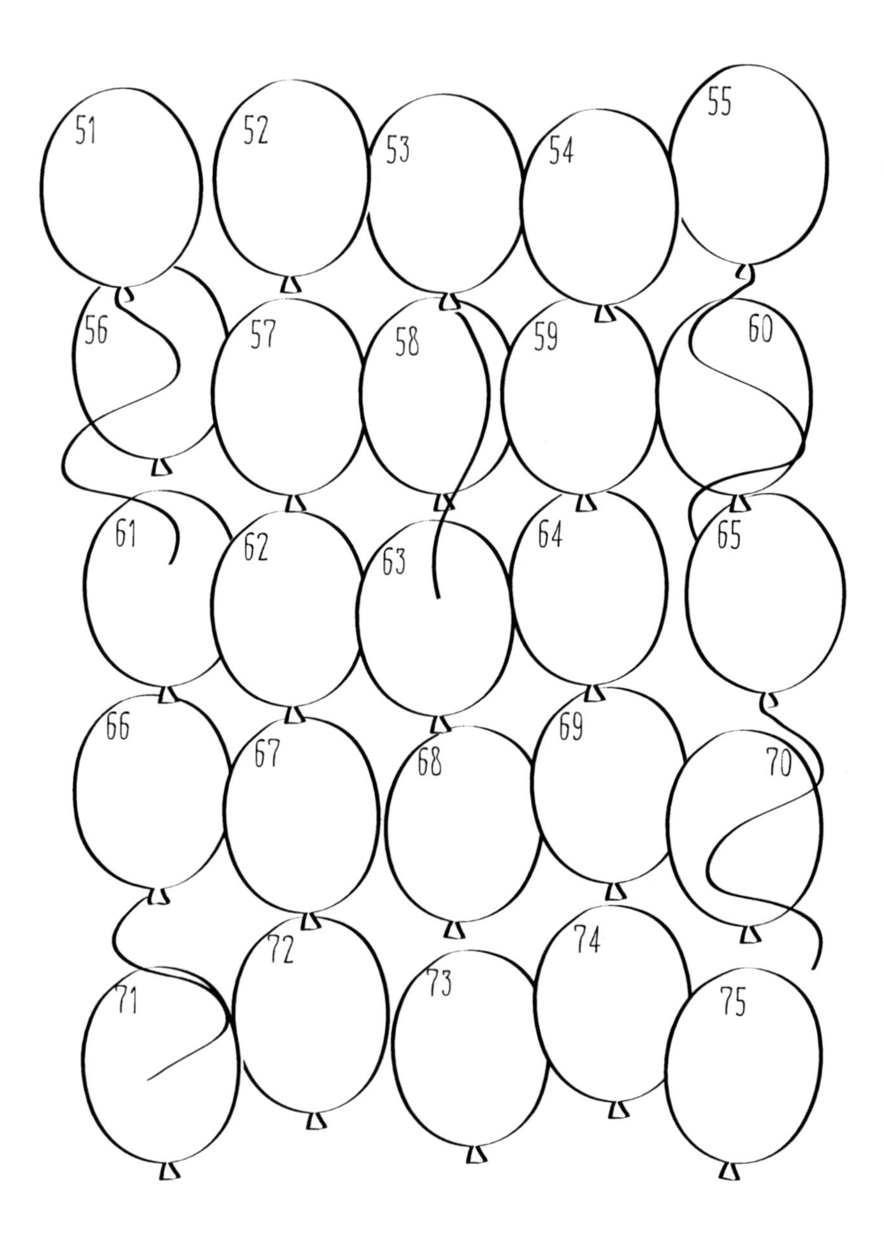
51
52
53
54
55
56
57
58
59
60
61
62
63
64
65
66
67
68
69
70
71
72
73
74
75

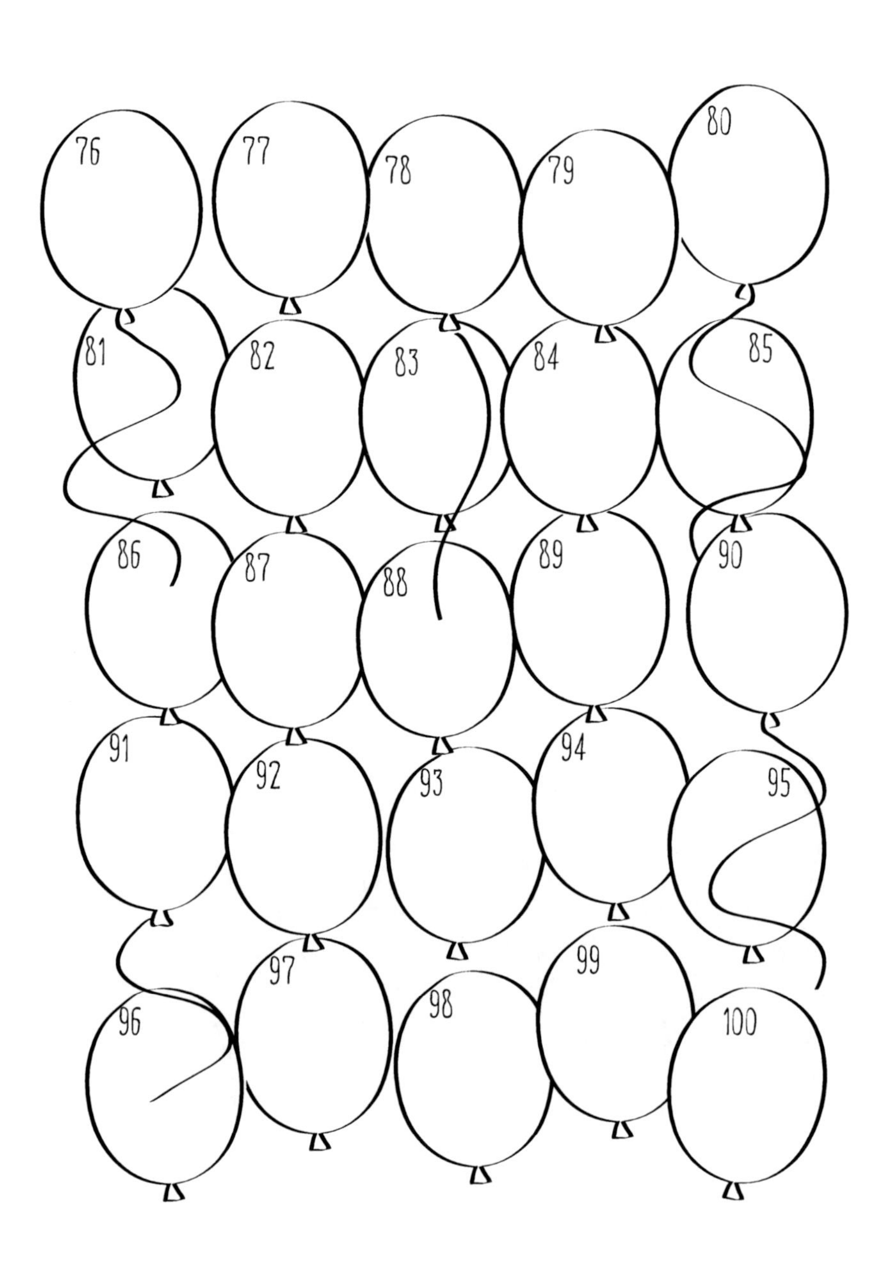
76
77
78
79
80
81
82
83
84
85
86
87
88
89
90
91
92
93
94
95
96
97
98
99
100

13. There is No Money In What I Do

I went into the business for the money, and the art grew out of it. If people are disillusioned by that remark, I can't help it. It's

the truth.

Charlie Chaplin

The market has no need for another actor or another painter/designer/didgeridoo maker. I am sorry if this comes as a surprise, but from a supply and demand perspective the market is more than saturated, and not that big in the first place. That's why the wages are bad until you become the person everyone wants, in which case you are rare and therefore valuable. They finally recognise that there is only one of you, and the money goes up.

My dad said that only the top 2% make a good living from acting. I have no idea where the figure came from but percentages always sound so official, and he's likely to have read it somewhere – it's my dad after all. I said, "Dad, that's fine, I just have to be in that 2%". Mission impossible? Maybe. Did you know scientists apparently found out that bumblebees can't fly? Their bodies are too big and their wings are too small in proportion. So scientifically speaking it's not possible! Lucky nobody told the bumblebees[4].

There is no money in the music industry is one of those commonly believed myths. I doubt Jon Bon Jovi would agree with this. Would Sting complain? There is no money in acting brings to mind the film *Notting Hill* where Julia Roberts, playing Hollywood actress Anna Scott, is at William's (played by Hugh Grant) little sister's birthday party. His brother-in-law, failing to recognise the film star, gives her the whole low-down on how hard it is to scrape by in the acting world. "Yeah, my friend is struggling on 8k a

---

4 Actually it's just one of those science jokes – this comes from 1934 when entomologist Antoine Magnan discussed a mathematical equation based on static aircraft wings, not wings in motion. Regardless, it's kind of a cute idea.

year". She smiles. "Where do you act mainly then?" "Films", she says. "Ah, yes, and what does the film business pay these days? I mean, how much did you make in your last film?" You can tell he's expecting to hear a number near the minimum wage. Her reply? "Fifteen million dollars".

YES! I love this scene because it whips us out of our expectations. There are plenty of multimillionaires in the acting, music and arts business. It's just that there are many, many more who never see much money at all. It may be true that your passion isn't feeding into a big market, and it may be well worth finding out what the situation really is. But chances are if you are passionate about something there may be others who are too. If you can find them and serve them, you have got a business.

Embarking on making money from your passion is an adventurous quest.

Maybe there is 'no money' in your passion but that isn't to say you cannot create a market around it. At the end of the day, that's what creatives are all about: we come up with new things. The Lumière Brothers didn't make the first ever film because there was a market. They had an idea and they must have had a great passion to turn it into a reality. Moving images did not exist but today they are a multibillion dollar industry we can't imagine living without. As far as I know the Wright brothers[5] didn't fly purely for the money (surely they could have found a safer way to

5 The Wright brothers, Orville (19 August 1871–30 January 1948) and Wilbur (16 April 1867–30 May 1912), were credited with inventing and building the world's first successful aeroplane and making the first flight on 17 December 1903.

generate an income) but their success founded the travel industry that feeds at least a hundredmillionthousandgazillionandfifty-fivepoint

three people.

So there is no money in your passion? Think again.

Be visionary. Be bold. You might as well.

Money isn't always in what you do. But it's certainly not in what you don't do.

14. Success decoded

You never
become a
howling success
just by

howling.

Bob Harrington

14. Success Decoded

What's your position on success? Doesn't the word sound wonderful and like what you really want? Success is one of those super-relative terms that get spun around and around to suit the needs of whoever is using the term. How do we define success? Often we are tempted to define it by the money made, which leaves little room for what I call authentic success: to do what you wanted to do.

And that may well include making money. Let's have a look at what the dictionary suggests:

1) The favourable or prosperous termination of attempts or endeavours.
2) The attainment of wealth, position, honours, or the like.
3) A successful performance or achievement: The play was an instant success.
4) A person or thing that is successful: She was a great success on the talk show.
5) Obsolete.

Origin:
1530–40 Latin successus, equivalent to succēd, stem of succēdere to succeed Related forms/Synonyms: achievement, fame, triumph (World English Dictionary)

Now I have to admit that, in my career as a performer, I enjoyed more success in the applause and validation segment than the financial one and, because my definition of success wasn't clear, I ended up very frustrated and confused. To the outside world I must have looked successful – to have shows up and running, an entourage, costumes and marketing. But in my little world I was stressed out, and worked hard to just make ends meet. What's successful about that?

Before we go any further, I would like you to take the time and find a definition of success that works for you. For me, the following thoughts ring true:

Success is:

- To do what I set out to do.
- When I have a good time.
- When I feel purposeful.
- Dancing with joy/excitement.
- Overstepping the confinements of my personal comfort zone.
- Being comfortable being uncomfortable.
- Sharing myself honestly.
- Being paid for doing what I love.
- Seeing others blossom.

Over to you: what is success to you?

1) ______________________________

____

____

2) ______________________________

____

____

3) ______________________________

____

____

4) ______________________________
____
____

5) ______________________________
____
____

6) ______________________________
____
____

7) ______________________________
____
____

My favourite revelation is this: success comes from succession, which is a biological term for further growth. The way vegetation evolves explains success the best. First we see a rock. No tree, not even grass, can grow on a rock – but lichen can and they will. They grow on the rock and then the biomass dies and another formation will grow on top. A moss seed flies along and can hang on to the lichen. The moss produces the soft green surface, which then transforms to the next level of moss, which organically evolves to become the foundation to the next until the moss is a squidgy and soft mass. That softness is nurturing earth on which grasses can grow. From the biomass of the grass there will be more ground, the perfect environment for a bush, then trees. You get the point.

Artrepreneur Principle 11:

Success is succession.

Have you noticed that many 'overnight success' stories have a long history behind them? Eddie Cantor, American singer, author and movie star of the 1930s, said "it takes twenty years to become an overnight success". The Beatles had played more hours together than most bands do in their entire career before they broke through. Find out how long those 'popping onto the scene' have already worked in the industry before we heard of them. Success is not a quick fix. Even Lady Gaga had been working in the industry for at least seven years before we got to hear of her. She started at age fourteen or fifteen writing hit songs for other bands, developing herself and her act.

Our past experience can fertilise our future. Seen in this context, everything you've done before, no matter how successful or not it was in the financial sense, or the sense of triumphing and achieving, can be used as the nurturing ground for whatever you choose to do next.

15. the f-words

Fear and Failure

Have no fear
of perfection.
You'll never

REACH it.

Salvador Dali

Carrie really wants to be a successful actress but when she doesn't get things right she thinks she may not be good enough. That's despite the fact that she got cast in the role and is brilliantly talented – which she forgets in those moments. This to me proves again what a great actress she must be to have such a powerful imagination as she can even pretend not to be successful when she clearly is. Wow. When she fears she is not good enough, she gets really anxious. Her concentration goes, she becomes shaky and she can even get quite depressed. That doesn't help with her acting, nor her motivation, nor her personal relationships, as you may well imagine. That in turn causes her more frustration and triggers the spiral downward to the den of despair. She then starts experiencing situations that 'prove' that she indeed isn't good enough.

We examined the thoughts that create those feelings. If you have been to therapy or read self-help books you may have learned to listen to your feelings and take your feelings very seriously. But what if feelings were merely the reactions of our body to our thoughts? Play with me for a moment: think about getting cast in a movie with your favourite film star. I just saw *Jerry Maguire* (yes, I know it's an old film) and I fancy Tom Cruise. So I am going to imagine being cast in a film with Tom Cruise! I am going to forget about his Scientology stuff and just think about the sexy charming character he'll play. I feel excited and giggly and a bit turned on. I just created that feeling!

Likewise when you think about something horrible (pick up the news if you need a dose of reverse inspiration) it's easy to feel really bad. We did an exercise at acting school (way back when) where someone whispered in our ear and we had to take it on as the truth and react. One time someone whispered to me, "Your mum just died, I am sorry". Within minutes I was sobbing uncontrollably. Then someone else said, "Universal Records want to sign you and your mum is fine – miracle recovery!" I was bouncing off the roof. Ready to buy everyone a drink!

Think about how you react. There is always a thought before the feeling. Sometimes we're not so aware of the thought – but that doesn't mean it's not there. We can trace it back, so why is this so ground-breakingly important? Because rather than taking Carrie to therapy to talk about her feelings and her childhood and her inadequacies, we can cut years of talking and find out that the thought that causes the anxiety is a chain of thoughts that boils down to this: I'm not good enough means I will be rejected by the world tribe and die in exile. If not being good enough equalled death you'd be reacting rather strongly to the possibility of not being good enough. You'd try to avoid it at all costs – even if the cost is your success.

So now we have looked at the validity of it all. I am not really interested, however, in whether Carrie is actually good enough or not, and that may differentiate me from most affirmative schools of thinking. Some people would have you jump up and down in front of a mirror telling yourself that you *are* good enough. You just need to convince yourself. But I think that's beside the point. Wouldn't it be really powerful to be independent of the momentary conviction? Because, you know what? Artistic Souls can be rather fickle. So what I believe passionately to be true today may not be the same tomorrow.

So why invest in a belief that changes all the time?

Much better to invest in being okay doing what you love no matter what!

Have I convinced you yet? Oh good. And if not – you don't need to be convinced, that was the whole point. Anyway – back to exploring the validity. Is it true that you (or my client Carrie) will die in exile if she isn't good enough? We agreed that no, that isn't actually quite so true now so before Carrie could launch into a "but why do I think it then? What's my problem?" I sneaked in this little review of our human development:

As a little child, you are dependent on your parents, the tribe, and other people taking care of you. This is why we grow up making sure we are accepted and we understand at a very deep level how important that is. But as an adult – things change. You are no longer dependent on the tribe to feed you and protect you – the rules have changed. This comes up again and again with my clients – sometimes we just haven't realised that the rules have changed. Being a grown-up is a very different ball game to being a child. Hurrah! Woohoo!

So if we don't die from not being good enough – could you relax? Now we know that when Carrie has her 'not good enough' thought, it's just that. A thought. A bit like "what's for dinner?" or "I don't like the smell of cigarettes". Who cares if you are good enough or not? That's not what it's about! What is it about? I hear you ask. I'm going to leave it to you to choose what it's all about for you. Maybe it's all about giraffes at the end of the day (sorry I had to bring it up again!)

My suggestion would be – and feel free to take it for yourself or have a completely different view – it's about doing what you want to do and doing it with all your heart and being. It's about liberating yourself. So what do you want to do? What would you do if you knew you couldn't fail? You know, the word failure is a bit loaded – it has a bit too much meaning. Actually it just means that you didn't do what you thought you would. It's not really a big deal unless you make it one.

A word on fear. Neale Donald Walsh is associated with the quote "Fear is an acronym for False Evidence Appearing Real". In other words, fear isn't real, it just feels that way. It's there to protect you from danger. When you are in real danger, you know it; it's a very specific kind of fear. Every person who's been in a real dangerous situation will testify that it feels different when a lion breathes on your face than when you worry about how you are going to pay your bills. There is a different sense to crossing a road and being surprised by a speeding car and thinking about not being liked by someone important.

Knowing that, I'd like to trust my own senses a little more. If I'm in "head fear" rather than acute danger fear I am willing to go on and through. There is a light at the end of the tunnel. And fear not. It's not the same light you'll see when you die.

It used to be my biggest fear to end up a failure. End up, is another one of these fantastically dramatic expressions. My partner Tom makes fun of me saying I must have learned them all in drama school.

Failing is good. Basketball player Michael Jordan teaches this powerfully – to goose bump level – in a Nike commercial (who would have thought?). He says he missed more than 9,000 shots in his career, lost almost 300 games, 26 times he's been trusted to take the game-winning shot and missed. "I failed over and over and over again in my life. And that is why I succeed."

Here is the link: www.youtube.com/watch?v=m-EMOb3ATJ0

I laughed when on my coaching course I was told, "There is no such thing as failure, there is only feedback". That's a very sweet way of consoling people. Sometimes I feel this positive thinking world is a bit of an escape from life. Let's not talk about failure and say feedback instead. There is no failure, only feedback – quite right. But sometimes the feedback is that you feckin' failed – say it in an Irish accent and it's even more powerful!

Come on, let's grow up and just say it. It's the new F-word! It's good for you. Amazing people fail. We were born to fail. Say yes to failure! Don't let them take your failure away from you! Stand up for your right to be wrong.

Sing with me to the melody of Rod Stewart in *Sailing*: I am failing... I am failing...

16. Working Hard

Versus Hard Work

Money doesn't talk, it

swears.

Bob Dylan

The truth is money can be made in many ways, including hard work, and many people who have made lots of money worked hard. But 'hard' and 'hard' are very different things.

Working hard isn't always a bad thing but when life becomes hard work we may want to stop for a minute and reflect. We might as well use our brain for a change for, as singer Sheryl Crow taught us, "I think a change... would do you good". You may by now be thinking "OMG, is she ever going to stop with her musical references on each page? My head is buzzing with songs I haven't heard in a long time and now this one."

Well, my friend, ever since I saw the Disney movie *Pete's Dragon* in 1981 I realised: life is a musical.

We think, we speak and then we break into song and dance. That's how it works. And everyone who hasn't got that yet, who is still stuck in the talking part of the show, better catch up quick because life is better that way. Plus, you get to choose your own songs. Life is a musical does not mean life has been written by Andrew Lloyd Webber. You don't have to *Starlight Express* yourself for the rest of your days – that's optional. Nor does life equal *Les Misérables* by Schoenberg/Boublil. In fact, to be less miserable, I'd recommend we use any songs that appeal, including our own. Woohooo!

Now back to the original topic, let me describe the three most common versions of 'hard' I've come across. I'm talking purely about work-related versions. You know what I'm saying.

Hard no. 1

"Oh, God, this is horribly hard! Argh." This is work that feels hard to you and is a real drag to do. It makes you feel exhausted just thinking about it. I am going to refer to it as **hard because you don't love it**. Maybe you don't even like it. Maybe you absolutely despise it more than words would dare to describe. This is hard with a vengeance.

We are talking about longer-term hardship, not just a task like having to get your taxes done once a year. Just get on with that, hard or not.

But if we are talking about a job that really goes against your likes and talents – about dreading getting out of bed because it's all so tough out there – that's hard no 1. Especially as creative minds, I urge you to realise that we have options, so create them and use them.

Hard no. 2

This is doing what it takes to get things done, whether you feel like it in the moment or not. It's about being a 'doer' instead of being a 'feeler'. Steve Chandler put it nicely when he observed: "Feelers can only do when they 'feel like it'. If there is a feeling that interrupts the good feeling, the motivation feeling, they will stop. Well, things don't necessarily get done this way. To be fair we've all succumbed to our feelings at some point or triangle."

A 'doer' will do, regardless of the feeling in the moment. A doer will recognise that the feeling follows our thinking and our action. Do the thing and you shall have the power! Do something amazing, and you will feel amazing. It's often quite simple like that. Hence working hard no. 2 is about **doing it**

no matter what. You want it, you get it done. It's good work. It can take time, it might make you sweat, it might be really hard, it might be outside the comfort zone but it is good stuff. It's making us proud. Yeaaah. Good hard work helps us have a good night's sleep afterwards. This is the only way of 'working hard' that makes any sense.

Hard no. 3

Here it is all about the image of hard work. It's the idea of working hard turned into a brand. It's all about the look. It's rather fashionable these days. But, as with many fashion fads, it's completely impractical and utterly useless. During my career in the corporate world, colleagues would go on about how hard they worked.

- "I stayed till 9:30 last night, I've got so much on!"
- "Oh, that's nothing, I've taken work home and had no weekend!"

It makes me want to beat them all with "I took the 20kg filing cabinet and slammed it on my toes whilst I was stabbing my eye and writing the reports with bleeding fingers. That's how hard I work for this company."

Working hard no. 3 is about **working hard to feed the image of being a hard worker.** Guess what, it's also the most ineffective way of working because working long and hard doesn't do anything. Well, it hurts, that's what it does. You don't get paid more because you suffered more. You don't do the job better because you had no sleep. The hit song didn't come because you slashed your wrists. So basically my colleagues were having a competition about how ineffective they were being!

Here is why we tend to believe in showing how hard we work:

From our early days at school, we wanted or needed to show the teacher how hard we were working. If you just smile and say the answer, the teacher will think it was too easy. Next thing you know they'd up the game till you've got to think hard and break into a sweat. In some cases, humiliation would follow.

At some point you learn to make the 'hard' face so you get away with less pressure or at least are taken seriously. At some point many start believing this effort is real and so

- They put their head down and work ever so hard.
- They start looking serious because that's 'professional'.
- They stop smiling.

At the office, I got into trouble for being in a good mood. My boss got a complaint because apparently a good mood meant I didn't have enough work to do. After all, my colleague in the same position but a different department was stressed out of her head! "Evelyne isn't working hard enough. She's having a laugh! What are we paying her for?" So my boss told me that I had to look a bit more serious to stop the rumours. "I know you're doing great but they see it differently and you know perception is reality." What a load of rubbish. I went to my desk and printed out my achievement list, a six-page document of the results I had produced. I tracked them deliberately at the end of each day. I got a pay rise and I kept my good mood.

When 'hard' becomes hard and vice versa:

129

Let's say you're going for what you want, whether it is calling Casting Directors or whoever is relevant in your field. Sometimes, often, we can get rejected as I know well since it took me three years and twenty-seven auditions to even get into acting school. "They said no! What am I supposed to do? They don't want me! This is hard!" It feels hard to keep going so it is easier to give up and many people do. If you're one of them, or ever have been, then welcome to the club. It's just what we do when we either don't know better or run out of resources. It's not always easy, is it?

It's not just in the arts that continuous diligence is needed to do well 'in the end'. Although unfortunately for too many artists doing well in the end was more 'after they died'. Any successful person knows that sometimes things get tough, but they didn't stop there. They had their mind made up and so they worked relentlessly and often put in a lot of hours. Sweated and pushed through any resistance and went beyond their comfort zone, beyond discomfort if necessary! That's what we mean with hard no. 2. It's what Darren Eden calls "being focussed on the end result". If you haven't created your end result yet, you refocus on what you want to see and take action on that.

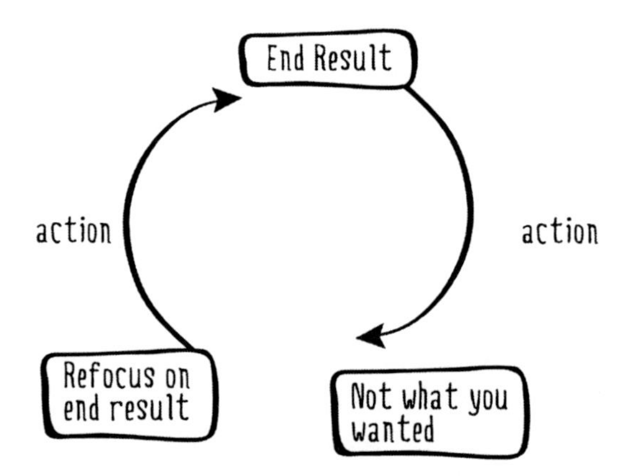

When you refocus on your end result and keep taking action, it's much easier to create it. However, that's not what most of us tend to do. Most of us tend to get sidetracked and go from the not achieving the desired outcome into a whole new world of evaluating what that means about us. For example: I wanted the gig, I sent out the CDs and I heard nothing back. What that means is that I am:

a) Not good enough.
b) Unlovable.
c) A worthless piece of poo.
d) Insignificant in this world.
e) Never ever, ever going to make it.
f) Better off getting a job in a video rental store.

So the list goes on. In Behavioural therapy, twelve core beliefs have been elicited that describe the main thoughts that get triggered and that we then buy into as truth, react to and essentially feel the consequences. But look at how egoistical this way of thinking is: something doesn't happen means

I am *** insert your own mental bullshit here**

I, I, I, me, me, me. No, it doesn't!!! All it means in my example is I didn't get the gig.

Best-selling author, spiritual teacher and speaker Dr Wayne Dyer when sharing about how he raised $40 million for public television to fund his TV series said, "Most people have a big list of things they would be willing to do in order to get what they want. But they equally have a big list of things they are not willing to do". His take is that the list of things we are not willing to do should be empty. Now I am going to add that Dr Wayne Dyer is a spiritual teacher and hence he probably assumes it's a given that you won't do anything immoral or against your values. But he is right that the more conditions we put on something to come into existence, the less likely we are to achieve it and the fewer conditions we put on something, the easier it is to actually get it.

His mission was to raise the consciousness of the American people and he knew that 'you need to be on TV to reach America'. Then he realised you don't need to be on TV to reach all of America, you can also go to all of America. Would you agree that is the hard way round? But that's exactly what he did. He travelled into each state where he lectured, raised people's consciousness and raised funds too – though to him that was a by-product. Travelling to each state – that's a lot of hard work.

Now I don't know about you, but I like an easy life. Or at least that's what I tell myself sometimes. So if you ask me, "Hey, Evelyne, do you want to run around the country playing in theatres every night in a different city dressed up as Madonna? Come on, it's going to be a FUN JOB!" I'd say no – it sounds like hard work and I don't want that any more. Not even if you paid me – though interestingly if you paid me a million I might think it was fun after all.

However, as Thomas noted, I've been working day and night building my coaching practice. I've been on it, out there, in there, studying, reflecting, connecting, transforming and writing. Me, the Queen of 'don't work overtime, life is about living!' which is what I told him when he was starting his company and working from 7am to 7pm for no salary. I said to him, "You don't have to work that hard – it's not good for you".

When you find something that makes a real difference to you and others then you are connected to your heart and you can find resources in yourself you didn't even think you had. I didn't work non-stop because I thought I had to in order to make the business work. It 'happened' because I loved it so much I booked more and more in. I know I have a great time when I coach so I made all my time about coaching.

Now let's get even more honest. When I talk about working a lot of hours on my coaching business, or working hard on something you love, is it really hard work? Does it even compare to working in a field for a day, or lugging around furniture for ten hours or listening to rape victims telling their stories? Hard work is relatively easy compared to really hard work. Hard work is a very relative term. I used to think that teaching singing was hard work because energetically and vocally I was drained after a day of it. But I just had to get used to it and build some stamina. Three years later I'd be teaching, performing and singing for eight hours and do a gig afterwards with no strain at all.

I find that in the 'glamorous' industries of music and theatre and the media world there is a tendency to work the longest hours, at the craziest times, for the worst pay, with the biggest dedication. It's almost as if there was a need to compensate for the fun it is to be part of a production. Given that media is very fashionable, there is probably a high consumption of the brand of hard work. Busting a gut in a tormented artist kind of way.

You don't work as hard as you can but as hard as you think.

Let's move from gut busting to myth busting: in our society being a hard worker is seen as a virtue. So not working hard can easily be read as being not as good a person. But is that true? Is someone who takes a break and enjoys himself or herself bad or is it simply that we feel more deserving when we really work for something? After all, we do value what we work for. A friend of mine who was doing well financially once said, "Well, I work hard for it so I deserve to be paid well". I thought of my mother who was bringing up two children on her own, doing night shifts and trying to pursue her path as an artist. After all, she'd studied graphic design and created beautiful artwork. Didn't she work hard too? Didn't she deserve more?

Here is another question to dismantle the myth of hard work = success: where did your most successful moments arise? Did they follow busting your gut or did some seemingly fall into your lap? You may find it's a combination of both. From my side I can say that my record deal with Sony Music wasn't me fighting for it. I took a job, met someone who introduced me to someone else who was a producer who liked my voice, who recorded me and sent it off to Sony. It was a chain of events, but not lots of hard work on my side. Having said that, I had been training and dedicating my life to being a great singer and performer so there was a foundation on which this success could flourish. I have clients who are being offered massive contracts as a result of a chain of creations and contacts and perfect fits for it. Not because they ploughed a field for a month at night whilst being tied to a log by one leg.

So in conclusion: Hard no. 1 (hard because you just don't love it at all) is just tedious, and the goal is to use your creativity to find a way around it. It's possible. Where there is a will...

Hard no. 2 (going for it whether you feel like it or not in the moment) is inevitable and some "I don't really like this" might come into play. The point is when we have a valid context, working hard for it isn't a problem, it's part of the game, even part of the fun. It's the challenges we grow from. It's the basis for the satisfaction we feel when we got it done.

Hard no. 3 (working hard to feed the image of being a hard worker) will present itself in varying proportion to your need for drama in your life. Join the revolution to create more effortless success.

17. How to Make Money From What You Love

Somebody said
to me, "But the
Beatles were anti-
materialistic".
That's a huge myth.
John and I literally
used to sit down
and say, "Now, let's
write a
SWIMMING
POOL".

Paul McCartney

Many people are stuck working for money instead of doing what they love. I also know plenty of people who go for what they love and make money and I want you to be one of us. There are people who follow what they love and end up pretty broke. Such as... oh yes, me again! Hello... most people who go for a dream don't usually get it served on a silver plate – or served at all. They are often seen serving plates to others in various bars and restaurants. Even Richard Branson almost went bankrupt a few times.

Today I saw Rhonda Byrne's new book *The Power*. She is famous through *The Secret* and in here she writes about the ultimate power: love. I couldn't agree more. I thought: dang, she's written my book! With a mixture of fascination, jealousy and curiosity I turned the beautifully printed pages until I got to the section where she writes about the connection between love and money. Apparently loving everything and sending love allows the law of attraction to operate and money stick to you. Apparently the more love you have the more money you get. It's a lovely idea but it is just not true. I've seen very loving people with no money and in fact that often seems to be the super-lovings' conflict number one. Now we could argue that when you love the conflict and you love your relationship with money and you love money and you love making money – then it may all come together quite nicely for you.

And in contrast, Pablo Escobar, the drug lord in Colombia, made $30 billion a year terrifying the world, killing those who got in his way, bribing the police and terrorising a country. He seems to have 'money stickiness'. Does he have a lot of love? Rich people are not automatically a great example of loving and grateful individuals.

Now I do like the idea of showing people how being a lovely person with lots of positivity will make you rich, and sending love to everything never hurt anyone – it's a good thing all round. It's just not the complete information and I really would love, love, love for you to have enough information to really make a huge shift in your life. So how does making money and doing what you love go together?

Very well, since you ask me. It is the best possible combination. I don't think that doing what you love has money following automatically. It certainly didn't when I did my music and cabaret performances. On the contrary, it was 'do what you love and work your socks, pants and bottom off to pay for it as well'. I do know that you CAN create money from doing what you love. There is more involved than love – although using love as the underlying energy is highly recommended and applauded! You will find the set-up and structure that allows money to come in – and clarity and focus around what exactly you are doing for whom – rather useful and crucial.

In the glamorous world of media, it's quite typical not to make much or any money even though lots of it is going around. In Paolo Coelho's *The Winner Stands Alone*, the rising star is dressed in designer clothes and paraded like a creature of luxury but behind the curtain she lives in a box room or with mum and dad because she is penniless. As an independent artist you may need to survive on a miniscule budget investing for a long time before you see the financial fruit of your labour, and not everyone gets a full harvest. You may need good survival skills for that time. This 'survival skill' is being financially responsible.

A friend of mine just got a deal to have his magic trick sold by a major production company. They will probably sell thousands of his DVDs and he probably won't see much money of that (if any) at all. It's not that he can't make money from what he loves, but he didn't set up a good deal. So the earlier you integrate the loving money mindset, caring about business set-ups too, the better. The less resistance we have to the business side of things, the easier it is to educate ourselves and negotiate properly. So maybe Rhonda Byrne is right after all. Just love everything.

Making money from what you love doesn't mean you *have* to make money from what you love. Just because you love something doesn't mean you *want* to make money from it. You may love painting but that doesn't mean you would like the profession of being a painter. You may love singing but you may not like the business of being a professional singer. I for example really don't like the working hours! You may love racing model boats on the pond but that doesn't mean your business idea of being a professional model boat racer is the most lucrative or satisfying. After all, running a model boat racing business involves a lot of tasks that may take you away from the actual racing. However, that is not to say it couldn't be great. What do I know about model boat pond races? Nada!

Making money from something you enjoy, though, can take the joy out of it. Many a diving instructor has lost their passion for diving right there on the job. I will be honest with you – I found this one really hard to understand for years because, to me, everything I did needed to be professional. I HAVE TO MAKE MONEY FROM WHAT I LOVE! I really identified with my career. Not making shit loads as a performer? Are you nuts? Do you know who I am?!?!

Life is a lot more fun and free since I understood that some things are better as hobbies.

And it's absolutely fine to have hobbies, things we love to do just for our enjoyment. I felt I had no time and no money for hobbies because I needed to get on with my career to make some money some day! Hobbies are for those who just can't take it to the next level? No. Hobbies are for those who choose to have fun in life. Hobbies are cool. Having said all that, it's also cool to extend a passion and create ways to make money from it. If that's what we want, let's go for it!

You may wish to grow what you love and expand it beyond one quirky activity such as, for example, sword fighting with wooden swords. Even with an eccentric thing like that you CAN make money. If there is someone else out there who loves it too and you can serve that person – woohooo. You can teach it; you can film videos about it and become a YouTube sensation and be approached by the company who produces wooden swords.

Nowadays it is actually possible to make money from just about anything! Take Danny McAskill. He rides bicycles across buildings, railings, and impossible obstacles. That's pretty unusual, right? That's his full-time job. If he had thought, 'Oh, I love doing crazy bike tricks but I can't because I have to make money' then he wouldn't have done it and we couldn't admire someone for something we would never do (wow!) and I couldn't share his glorious example here. But this guy loved doing the bike tricks so he did more of it and he became extraordinary. And a bicycle company is now paying him to ride their bikes.

Being extraordinary at what you do is certainly a good pointer to success. It also goes with our artistic values to be brilliant. It would make sense that an amazing pianist makes more than a mediocre one. But here's the crux: it's not a given. You can be a wonderful pianist and not make a penny. There are amazingly talented people out there who are poor. They'll probably say they are poor because they are so busy playing they don't focus on the money, or they blame the world for it. My mum's ex-partner was probably one of the world's best clarinettists. I can say that because this guy was in his sixties and plays the clarinet daily, spending four hours practising his instrument, the scales, the intonation, the sheet music. He has been doing that all his life. I have not seen a more dedicated musician in my life. He turned down orchestra work because it would keep him from his art. He preferred to improve. You can imagine he wasn't well off. He taught at a small music school. He didn't believe in the system of the academies because they don't understand what makes a true artist. This guy was and still is all about his music. That didn't make him 'successful' in the classic sense. But he lives his dedication to art. He doesn't get to live with my mum any more though... he is married to his clarinet.

Madonna isn't known to be the best singer in the world. She's no Maria Callas, Christina Aguilera, Mariah Carey, Barbra Streisand... but she doesn't need to be. She isn't known as the best songwriter either. Although, credit to her, she's written a string of memorable hit songs lasting through the ages – something most people definitely can't say about themselves no matter their reputation. I love how we sometimes feel compelled to criticise those who are doing very well. Madonna is exceptional at getting in with the people on the edge, she's great at business, she is a phenomenal worker. She has mega discipline, focus, dedication, will. She knows how to create results more than most. She has mental power. Some people like to say Madonna isn't a real artist because she is highly commercial and she is very much into her business. Let me point out, she studies all forms of art deeply; she is incredibly well educated and well read in art. She has trained extensively in dance, music and art history to reference in her shows. She is in control of everything concerning her career. She is very much an artist – she expresses herself through her art in an accessible art form. She is a pop artist. For her, money and art go together very well indeed.

Madonna is on the money in all areas. I have studied Madonna intensively through my work as her impersonator/ tribute and I have always had mixed feelings about the way she's built her career. I admire that she has produced so many outstanding results but I wouldn't want to be like her. I am aware that, though I've studied what is said about her, that doesn't really mean I know her as a person. So my perception is not a hundred percent pure. I can say for sure though that the extreme lifestyle is not what I am looking for. It took me a decade to realise that.

So how do we do it then? Making money doing what you love comes down to finding the sweet spot at which you do something you love for which other people are prepared to pay you money. Chris Gillebeau points out, "Naturally, you won't get paid for everything you love, but there is usually a sweet spot of convergence between what you love and what people want to pay for". Clay Collins[6] illustrates this concept well with the following diagram adapted from Chris Gillebeau's *279 Days to Overnight Success*.

---

6 Clay Collins www.marketingshow.com.

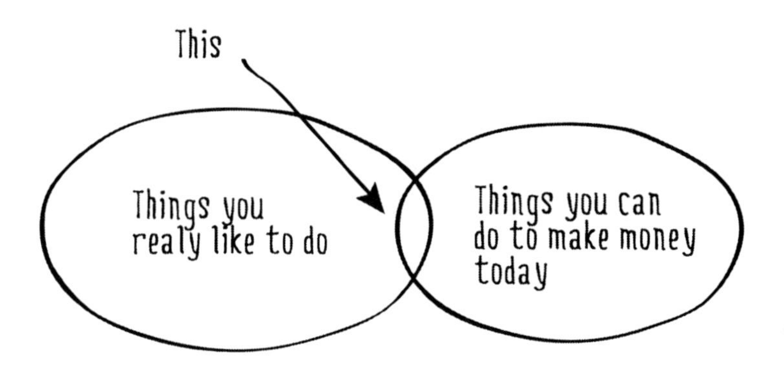

I like to sing ballads the way Eddie Fisher does and the way Perry Como does. But the way I'm singing now is what makes the money.

Elvis Presley

Artrepreneur Principle 13:

Making money from what you love is based on the sweet spot encompassing what you love and what other people pay for.

So here is how you make money from what you love in a generic nutshell.

- Find out what you love.
- Find out what people are happy to pay you for.
- Elicit a sweet spot.
- Create the service/product around that.
- Let people know about it – tell them what's in it for them.
- Ask for money in exchange for your service/product.

There is no need to get religious about this. Keep it simple and sweet! And remember you don't have to make money just from what you absolutely love. It may be a great idea to make money from what you are good at making money from and support what you love through that. Let's say what you love isn't a money making thing. Take for example kayaking or travelling or writing songs that don't fit in the well known structures of pop or jazz... and you'd rather enjoy that than get frustrated with record industry demands or the workload of indie distribution. Why LIMIT your income sources to your big passion?

Doing something just for the money, because you need the money, because you want the money can feel empty and like self-betrayal. It's the number one conversation I remember having with my classmates at A-level time. Do you remember that time when we ended school and the big question was, "What are you going to do?" and whereas some had grand plans, clear ideas, others were completely lost. And then there were those who said, "Well, I'll study business or go into banking because at least there's money in it". Goose bumps of horror would form on my body. How could anyone devote their life to something so shallow?

And now, years have gone by since those days and discussions whether one should make money or do something for the love of it. The same discussion remains true yet many more will have joined the ranks of, "Well, you've got to do something to pay the bills. You've got to make compromises." Am I suggesting you should compromise on your passion to go for the cash? No. That's not what I am talking about. Because a compromise is the resignation to 'okay' and giving up on 'great'. It does not come with the energy of love, freedom and Creative Power. I'm not a big fan of compromise. Are you?

I want to offer you to make choices. Making choices is powerful[7]. "I choose to make money" is not a compromise. It's not saying "I'd really rather travel the world in a circus but teaching kids will do for now. I have no choice on

---

7 *What Happy People Know*. In this book Dan Baker PhD talks about working with depressed patients. Making simple choices brings back a sense of personal power and control.

this. I have a baby and the baby needs feeding. I have responsibilities, you know, so I can't just do what I want. ... Oh, well."

"I choose to make money" has much more power behind it. It is saying for example, "I make my choice based on what is truly important to me. Being with my own child at the moment is the most important thing to me. I love my baby. I love the excitement and the challenge and the bond we have as a family. In a few years' time I might travel with the family and join the circus, who knows? But for now this is what suits us best. Sometimes it pushes all my buttons at once and I will say I hate it but, really, I love it."

Being powerful in your life is not a result of luck or circumstance. Like making money, it becomes a choice. When we feel powerful, we feel happier and freer in ourselves. Freedom is the key!

18. How to Ask

For Money - Or Charging Made Easy

Whoever said
money can't
buy happiness
didn't know
where to shop.

Gertrude Stein/
Bo Derek/Gittel Hudnik

For Artistic and Soul-centred individuals, asking for money isn't always second nature. It's more seventh nature or no nature at all. We love the idea of someone buying our painting, CDs, or booking us for a gig but we don't necessarily want to talk about the money side. Why not, actually?

What's so bad about money? What's the hiccup?

Your CD is of value to someone else. Music can change the world, right? How often has a song in your head changed your mood, your day, or provided a valued and cherished memory? So you not selling that CD means not giving someone the opportunity to have that memory with your music. And trust me, it's sooo cool when you hear that someone is having special moments with your music. For example, I didn't know for years that my song 'Smelly Armpits' has been sung very loudly in some living rooms getting teenagers to laugh at the world. Now, thanks to YouTube and Facebook, fans have come forward and told me about it. If you want to hear it, go to iTunes or Amazon for Diva Eve: Smelly Armpits. We have to give people a chance to have a good time with our music/book/acting/passion!

You are adding value to the world.

A great way to ask for money is to be straightforward, open-hearted and do it with clarity. Keeping it simple is the key and here's the process: you set up a fee or your price and you name it. Just as you would say your telephone number if someone asked you for it. We don't go "Errm, I don't like talking about numbers... that's the difficult part, gosh, it's relative, what's your number approximately? Are you in the 0207 or 01203 prefix?" How do you start? "I guess I'm somewhere between 1 and 10 to start with and then 6 or 7..."

No, you would just say your number and you don't ask afterwards if that is okay. That's how you ask for money. If I have a product, I make up a price for that product. If you have a service, set up a fee for that. It is just like having a phone with a telephone number - it goes hand in hand. You don't say 0207 12345679 and then go, "Is that alright? I can change it if you want?" But many do say a price and then make a face to show they are not comfortable with it. "Is that alright, £40 for an hour's treatment? Or if it's too much, I'll do it cheaper." You wouldn't do that with your phone number, so don't do it with your fee number.

And remember you can change fees just like people have been known to change their phone number. It's legal.

Fees hold no meaning. They are simply numbers.

Now, wait a minute. What's your fee based on, how do you set the right fee? I hear you ask. (Call me Joan of Arc with my voices... but don't burn me later!) So, are there rules for setting fees? There probably are and I recommend you break them as quickly as possible.

18. How To Ask For Money - Or Charging Made Easy

If there was one principle here without which making money is impossible it is this: you need to ask for it.

It is very rare indeed that people come up to you and say "I want your CD and I'll give you €20,000 for it". It's more likely they come up and say, "I will give you €2". We need to ask for the money. Asking not as in please, please can I have €10? Asking in the sense of stating your price with confidence. There are two ways of setting fees: Business-based or Heart-based

1 Business-based

This means you look at the market, you look at the demand for your product or service in that market and you set your fee according to that. You may wish to conduct market research to find out what the people you want to work with actually want and like and how much they would be prepared to spend. Market research, for those with business phobia, is just a fancy way of saying you ask people and find out what they think.

Take a music CD by an unknown singer, budget production, and at the time of writing it sells for £5-£10 per CD (in the UK). If it were burned at home, I would expect a lower price, but is there a demand for it? Not unless you're known or you give a concert and build a reputation. But it's easy to set the price because CDs all cost around the same.

A painting is different: it can be £10, £100,000 or a few million (no matter where and in what currency). Who decides how much a painting is worth? Of course, if you are known, your price may be higher but generally speaking it's challenging to go about it in the business way. First off finding your market for the painting and then asking what it would pay – how could you know? It all depends on too many factors. When my mum tried to price her paintings, she got all sorts of smart advice. Some people said she had to be expensive so that people would value the painting, but the problem was she felt really embarrassed talking about a high price. She felt that she was just making it up and people might laugh at her, and it felt as if she would be fleecing people. She didn't sell any pictures, so what's the point of having a high price if no one buys? Then some people said, "Well, obviously if no one buys it means your price is too high! You have to lower it!"

I remember my partner saying I should lower my performance fees when I didn't get enough gigs. So I called round and lowered my fees and told my agents that I was going down in price to get more jobs. Do you want to know how much more work I got? Zilch. Nada. Nothing. Just because it's cheaper doesn't necessarily mean you will sell more. You could – but it's not guaranteed. But guess what? The few gigs I got were for a lower fee, so all in all it really meant less money! I put my prices back up and interestingly I still had little work but it wasn't that much of a problem because at least it was well-paid. Why was it well-paid? Because I ASKED for the money. Some would argue that it all comes down to self-worth and self-esteem and self-confidence.

We could spend some time discussing this; we could simply say that it comes down to asking for the money regardless of all that stuff. Often you'll find that confidence is a result of your actions and your self-esteem issues dissolve into pleasant pride when you take action on your life and do what you truly believe in. Sometimes we need a little nudge

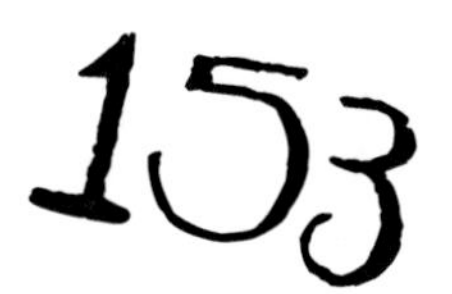

first. But most of the time we just need to make our mind up and nudge ourselves. If you'd like to read in more detail about confidence and what it's made of, feel free to request my 'Claim Your Confidence' guide from my website www.brinkcoaching.co.uk and I will send it as my gift to you.

2 Heart-based

When it comes to performance fees, paintings, services, we need to have a look at the Heart approach. I learned this from Supercoach Michael Neill and Reiki master Sabine von Neubeck in Berlin. Here is how it works: you put your hand on your heart. You think of someone who loves you or someone you love until you get all fuzzy and warm inside. Then you ask: how much is my painting worth? I did this with my mum and she said, "I don't know". This is how the exchange went:

Is it €5?
No!!
Okay, is it €5,000?
NO!
Okay, is it €3,000?
No.
Higher? Lower?
Lower.

And we did that until she had a number that felt right for her. Hand on heart it usually takes five minutes to get your heart-fees. Now guess what? My mum has been selling considerably more paintings and started living from that income. She can go out and ask for the money because she knows it's the right price. It's in tune with her heart.

It's so much easier to ask for what you believe in.

I am a big fan of heart-based pricing, having experienced it myself for the first time when I took my Reiki initiation. Sabine was going to spend two days with me to teach me one-to-one. I said, "I am a student, I hardly have money, how much will it be?" She put her hand on her heart and said, let me feel it, and then decided it was DM300 (this was in pre-Euro times, can you imagine?) When I said, "Can you make it cheaper?" she said, "No, that's the price that feels right". Inside myself I could feel that too and it was alright so I accepted it. It's funny how I said, "I have no money" but I said yes to it because it was important to me and I came up with the money and I knew it was the right thing to do. I had no time for all the silly thoughts about not being able to afford it and "What would Dad say if he knew I did Reiki? Am I totally bonkers?" that usually infested my thinking.

When you set your prices based on your heart, you know you are true to yourself.

"But how do I know I will get that money?" It's really simple. If you add enough value, someone will want it and they will find the money. My Reiki master didn't know if I would give her that money, after all I was a student, but it was important to me. She was amazing and the time felt right, so I took it from my savings. People spend money on all sorts of things for all sorts of reasons. Sometimes for important things that transform their lives, but more often on drinks and nights out that are forgotten quickly, consumer goods, fleeting experiences. Billions are spent on things we don't even need.

And billions are spent on things that, when we reflect back, we never really wanted.

If you have something of value – offer it. If you want money, you need to ask for it.

19. do you Like Money?

Money is not the most important thing in the world. Love is. Fortunately,

i Love Money.

Jackie Mason

We talk about wanting more money because we have dreams to fulfil for which we use money: from buying a lovely flat to amazing holidays, from buying rounds to inviting your girlfriends to the spa or your man friends at the bar after driving that racing car (poetry slang, friends, did you notice those witty rhymes? Car bar spa – incredible).

Many of my dreams also have a price tag. If you asked me, "Do you like money?" I'd say, "Yes, of course, what's not to like about money?" But when I look at how I have lived my life I find another belief playing out which is an 'it's got to be right' belief around money. I get really suspicious about people who have a lot of money. How did they get it? I wonder. Did they do it in the right way or did they do some dodgy stuff?

As I mentioned at the beginning, I admire people who really earned it and who 'deserve' it by my high ethical standards. I feel that Oprah, who created such a powerful and inspiring platform and helps so many people through her work, totally deserves endless wealth. Louise Hay who founded Hay House Publishing - of course she should be rich! But what about people marketing on the Internet or at seminars? My partner Thomas has noted that much of the information I got at seminars for which I paid thousands of pounds I could have read in books at £10 each. But to me, being with people in a live situation in a room with the author of the book increases the learning experience enough to justify the increase to the higher price. It is not about what you pay, it is about the value you get from it.

This is what I don't like about money:

- The expectation to deliver on a job and do things that you don't like because the money is good.
- If money makes you do things you don't want to do.
- If money means taking away from others I'm not a fan.
- If money means doing unethical things to get it, I'm not impressed whatsoever.

But really, what I am doing is linking money to doing things I don't want. Remember money doesn't mean anything until we make it mean something (ARTREPRENEUR Principle 8). What about crime? Aren't most crimes committed because of money? People are killed for money and they go nuts because of money. George Bernard Shaw said it so beautifully: *Money is not the root of all evil. The lack of money is*. I'll go a step further and add that the belief that money means more than *you* is the root of all evil.

When we adapt our behaviour to money, worship it, turn our thoughts and lives around it, and sacrifice ourselves for money, that's when we are in trouble.

And I am guilty as charged. I have spent sooo much time worrying about it throughout my life. "What should I do? Will I ever have it? What if I'll always be poor?" Plus the associated nasty feelings that come with thinking about not having enough and not knowing how to get it. This is why I am so passionate about clearing up the confusions on the topic. The pain is so unnecessary! We've been educated to believe that money makes us happy. But if it were true every investment banker would be skipping down the street on a daily basis.

Robert Holden, PhD.'s story of his father is a powerful testament to this: One day rushing to see friends he passed a man lying face down on the street. Though everyone was walking by pretending not to see him- for all they knew he could be dead- for some reason Robert stopped. Cautiously he turned to the dishevelled drunk, turned his face around only to recognize his own father.

Before living on the street this man was what everyone would have considered very successful. He held senior positions in investment banking, had a great family, a nice house. How could someone who truly had it all (including a son who'd turn out to be one of the most amazing teachers of wisdom and love) fall so low?

The answer is as simple as it is profound: Things aren't always as they seem.

What looks like success to you and me is not necessarily what goes on inside. And we experience our life from our inside, not from the perception of others.[8]

Money neither makes you happy nor can it buy happiness. You might feel happy when you buy something – but it's short lived. Harvard University Social Psychologist Dan Gilbert says, "We think money will bring us lots of happiness for a long time when in fact it brings us a little happiness for a short time"[9]. And it still holds true that – as even The Beatles

---

8 Robert Holden PhD.: Success Intelligence page, prologue

9 Carey Goldberg, "Too much of a good thing", *Boston Globe*, 6 February 2006 (quoted in Sonja Lyubomirsky, *The How of Happiness*).

pointed out – money can't buy you love. Money can't buy you happiness – but then again, you wouldn't ask a fridge to walk. In other words, let's use money for what it's good for and let's not judge it for what it's really not good for. Money is useless at buying happiness and love. Fridges are useless for walking and making coffee. If you want to go for a lovely walk in the countryside, don't wait for your fridge to come with you. Learn from my mistakes, honey, you're wasting your time.

We have established that liking money really helps for making more of it because there is no point creating what you don't like in your life. So are you ready to get clear and clean in your feelings towards money? Then let's detox, de-clutter and spring clean your mind. You are hereby also cordially invited to do the same for your fridge but that's optional.

Here is a powerful exercise I'd like to share with you:

Write down ten pages about what money means to you. It may sound like a lot but it's what you're going to want to give yourself so you can go beneath the surface of "Hey, I am okay with money, really! This sounds like a lot of work. I only have a couple of things maybe, but seriously, I'm fine!" That's how we avoid finding the gem, so allow yourself to go on a journey through your conscious, and unconscious, mind and see what gets revealed when you get stuck in and shine the torch of awareness on to the topic.

The goal of this exercise is twofold: to get clean of your negative thoughts around money and clear about your positive thoughts around money. The way we can learn to like money is by looking at all the negatives and realising they are just made up. So are the positives by the way. We make up the meaning of things. Money is just what it is, but how we think about it makes all the difference in our life!

Being clear and clean about money helps us create money effortlessly. There is no point in creating something we don't like.

This next exercise will help you with that.

Brain Drain exercise:

Work through each of these statements one at a time and write down everything you can think of. When you can't think of anything else, that's blank point number one and just keep going because there will be more. You want to pass two blank points to wring out your brain for all the most absurd thought combinations you hold in there.

Then move on to the next statement.

Start with: Money means... (and continue)
Not having money means.... (and continue)
My issue with money is... (continue)
I wish money was... (continue)

And write down everything. This exercise serves two major purposes: first to look at what we are thinking and get it out. Detoxify the brain. Second, to create the distance between our thoughts and the belief that they are real. It's easier to 'see' our thoughts when they are written out on paper. Sometimes a child will draw a monster and then get scared by it. That's exactly what we do when it comes to our thoughts. We think them and then get scared of the monster. Playing the brain drain can help you look at the monster for what it is: thoughts.

Please don't skip this step. I know it feels good to just read a book and move on. If you are anything like me, the good feeling is satisfactory enough and can leave you skipping the required action to create real change. Unless you read this just to feel a little better, please do yourself a favour, give yourself the gift of real change! I've read countless books on how to get rich and not made a penny afterwards because I didn't follow through on them. Why didn't I? I couldn't be bothered or I thought, "I got it – thanks, I'll do that!" But I don't "do that". If it's not about transforming someone's life or recording a new song I just wrote, or doing something extremely romantic with Thomas, chances are I'll put it off for another time.

Which proves the point that you need:

The Big WHY

We need a really good reason. A purpose. I suppose, given that you are reading this book you have a good reason to give your current money mindset an overhaul. We did the hundred reasons to create money exercise earlier – so you have got a hundred good reasons by now. What I would love for you is the most simple reason ever: because I want to. Michael Neill also writes about making money a worthy goal. When you look at what would make money a worthy goal for you, it's much easier to create it. The thing is, we are not really after the money so much, are we? As Artistic Souls, we tend to have other things on our mind... and because of that, do it NOW.

20. Living Within Your Means

I'm living so far
beyond my income
that we may
almost be said to
be living

APART

E. E. Cummings

The reason many of us despise money is that we feel it dictates our life in terms of what we can and cannot afford. The really nice things can seem unavailable when outside our budget. Research suggests that money makes a difference in happiness levels only up to a certain point[10]. If you are below a mid-range salary, I can relate to budget frustrations and your focus is well served by learning to generate more. However, understanding that we don't really need that much helps us build our freedom and peace around this topic. If I'm not looking for millions to live my happy life but just for £47,000, it's a little weight off the shoulders.

Also what helped me a lot on this journey was to recognise that the happier I am in myself, the less I need. My desire for buying stuff is much less now than it was ten years ago and that certainly helps me live within my means. I remember buying my sister a wonderful make-up pen to remove dark circles under the eyes. I thought: I need one of those! I'd look so much better so should I go and buy one? Then it dawned on me that sleeping also takes care of dark circles and you don't have to pay for it – another feel-good factor.

Sometimes I see amazing clothes and am tempted to think how great they would make me look. I know now that if I want to feel beautiful, a run, yoga session or dancing will have an even more powerful effect. It's not what you wear; it's how you wear it... So living within our means is not about restricting yourself like crazy but to look at what you have and

---

10 A study in the US in 2010 found that earning more than US$75,000 a year (a bit less than £50,000) did not contribute significantly to well-being.

what you want, then asking yourself: is there another way to get it that doesn't cost (or doesn't cost as much)? If we can have it for nothing, i.e. looking good/better, then why spend money on it?

However, sometimes you do want to spend money – there are friends to be visited, journeys to be journeyed, fun to be had! Some clothes are great on you so why shouldn't you get them? To create a wonderful life, we need to know where we want to go AND where we are now. That part can be sobering and that is where true power lies. The mind shift we want is to switch from thinking about what you don't have, can't afford and don't want to see, to openly embrace your current reality and your vision and be able to see the gap between them. That's the point.

Now instead of going, "Oh, noooo, my reality doesn't match my vision, poor me" and crying yourself to sleep, I'd like to offer you a new of way of thinking about it:

If there wasn't a gap between your current reality and your vision, you'd have no space to create.

If you wanted to draw a picture but then instead of a blank canvas I gave you one with your picture already on it, would you be happy? Of course not! You wanted to draw the picture and you need the blank paper to paint your picture. We want there to be a nice gap between what we have got now and what we want because that establishes the space in which we can create. Creating is fun; it's our human instinct so that taking away creating from humans is like taking off the brown spots from a giraffe.

21. ANYONE STILL Resisting The Numbers?

If you really want something in this life, you have to work for it. Now quiet, they are announcing the LOTTERY numbers

Dan Castellaneta
for Homer Simpson

I remember a session on money with a wonderfully creative client of mine who wanted to master her finances, so I asked her to fill out a document stating exactly how much she made and spent. I also asked her to mark her spending in order of priority: fixed costs, variables, and costs she could actually avoid. She would use her bank statements to see what was going out. The following week I asked her about this assignment and she hadn't done it. "I just can't get myself to fill it out." So we did it together and, to her surprise, she actually enjoyed the process and the clarity it brought for her. She felt hugely empowered by seeing exactly what she was doing and could make some clear decisions.

Most people I know want to be in control of their financial situation but very few are taking the appropriate actions.

If you want to master money, you must take action. You have to actually deal with your reality. Reality gets a bad reputation for being harsh and biting but actually it is also the place in which our power and all the real possibilities live. Many people feel a sense of fear when thinking about their numbers. What if they are worse than anticipated? Isn't it better just not to know? Ignorance is bliss, right? Is it really? Does it hurt less when the debt collector rings your bell? Most of the time we paralyse ourselves with thoughts about what may happen and fall back on the superstition that somehow not knowing about it will mean we won't have to deal with it. The 'ignorance is bliss' principle has been practised far and wide and, if you ask me, is the foundation of the recent financial crisis in the world.

Was ignoring the iceberg really helpful for the *Titanic*?

Do you know the difference between ignorance and indifference? Answer: I don't know and I don't care. I love it when we say, "I don't care". I've noticed that, at least for me, that's not even true. I do care. I care a lot. I care about life and love and well-being. I care about being happy. I say I don't care about money but my life is determined by how much I don't have, so of course I care. Money affects us in other areas of life about which we very much care, so let's face it. Let's CARE. Care is what is going to help us look at what we are doing and learn from it.

When Michael Neill asked me to write down how much I wanted to earn in a month, he asked for three numbers:

- What I'd need to survive.
- What I'd like.
- What would be amaaazing.

I'll be honest with you: I wanted to just jot three numbers down and be done with it. There you go! That's my goal, now help me achieve it! But Michael wanted to know what those numbers meant to me, and what they were based on, because a random number as a goal is not a very strong motivation. Why would we walk a rocky road towards a goal we are not strongly motivated about? Motivation means we find something really important. When I ran down the Andes mountains in Peru, and please don't try this at home, it was a risky thing to do. The path was rocky, I was on my own and in danger of falling or getting lost, apart from not getting enough oxygen due to the thin air. You shouldn't run down the Andes mountains and you certainly shouldn't do it alone. I didn't do that for a random number that didn't mean much to me. I did that because the life of my loved one was at risk. He was very ill and being carried at amazing speed by local farmers. I did what I could to be by his side, praying all along life would be kind to us. Had you asked me if I could even do this, I would have been rather doubtful. No sleep, no food, little to drink, on my own, with my ankles that are famous for twisting? Can I pass? But when something is close to our heart, we stop asking, we stop doubting, and we jump into action as though there was no tomorrow.

We are motivated by meaning. Let's make the numbers mean something really cool.

We need to identify a meaning for the numbers. That's what I did to find out what achieving my three financial goals would actually mean in my life. So I sat down and wrote on a spreadsheet what I wanted the money for: rent, bills, mobile, Internet, travel, theatre, cinema, going out with friends etc. Then I divided the 'needs' from the 'wants' so I could see what the minimum number was I needed, where the good life begins and where luxury takes over. In order for me to have more fun with it, I coloured my spreadsheet because we can make looking at numbers a pleasure. If looking at numbers means excruciating pain doing what you hate – then it would be hard to motivate yourself. But if it means that's the time you get to make your favourite tea, and you schedule a pampering treat every time you do it, I bet your attitude will change.

It's worth reprogramming the connection you make to looking at your numbers, so now it's time to be playful. Think about it as a game you are learning to play in which winning will really benefit your life and losing is simply a nudge to learn more. Why did my client find it easy and fun to fill out her forms with me? Because money is one of her blind spots, something she's quite successfully ignored for a long time, and her habit is to ignore. When I asked her and looked over her shoulder, she found herself doing it and actually enjoying it. Some things are best done with someone who cares.

Students have been found to improve at subjects they struggled with when a teacher came along who **cared.** Who cared enough to take the time to walk them through. Here is a story about how deep caring for someone transformed their life.

There was a little boy at a school in a little town in a little country called Germany whose mother had passed away. He became very sad and didn't interact much any more. In fact, he became quite disruptive and untameable. His migration background meant that his language skill was poor and as the story goes his schoolwork dropped below the basic level. He had been passed from class to class and all the other teachers in the school had given up on him as a child too difficult to deal with. A hopeless case. The school council deemed his case unsolvable. "I'll take him on," said Gudrun Oppenheim, a teacher at the school. Everyone sighed in relief. One person crazy enough to take the burden off their shoulders! Gudrun liked a challenge and she didn't believe in hopeless. On the first day she saw him, she took him to one side and said to him, "I want you to know that you are very special to me. You are my birthday present this year. I got you in my class for my birthday and I would like to make this a very special year. Thank you for being in my class." The little boy was not used to that treatment. He soon warmed to his new teacher, who gave him attention, asking him how he was and helping him out. He started to thrive and become a calmer and happier kid. His performance improved. When Mrs Oppenheim returned from a week off being ill, he ran up to her and welcomed her with a big joyous hug. Not only was the mission of making him a better student successful, this human being had learned to deeply care.

If you feel you need someone to care with you about looking at your numbers, get yourself an action buddy. A friend who wants this too, who you can hold accountable and who holds you accountable. Or of course, hire a coach!

PS: Gudrun Oppenheim is my aunt and this little boy is one of many she blessed with her love, skill and energy.

The magic of transformation lies in deep care.

Care to see for yourself? Here are some carefully selected exercises:

The three magic numbers[11]

1) Find out your 'need to survive' number.
   Add up the costs that you must cover to live. That's your survival sum. This will include:
   - Rent/mortgage
   - Food
   - Travel costs
   - Utilities
   - Telephone
   - Mobile/cellphone
   - Internet
   - Basic health/hygiene/household products
   - Buffer (for the little stuff you didn't account for)

2) Find out your 'I can live with that' number.
   By adding your basic costs, plus everything that makes up a life you can live with (i.e. also insurances and basic savings).

3) Find out your 'amazing life' number.
   By adding up living costs, the things that make life good, and money to fund your amazing life style.

Share and compare with your action buddy and/or coach.

11 This exercise was introduced to me by Michael Neill.

The Reality Checkmate Game

1) Make yourself a cup of your favourite non-alcoholic drink.
2) Schedule time out – thirty minutes to an hour.
3) Make yourself very comfortable.
4) Turn on some relaxing music – optional.
5) Create a spreadsheet.
6) Take your last bank statement and write down everything you spent and what category it belongs to: such as household, fun, travel, office, luxury, health, pampering etc.
7) Add up the amounts per category.
8) Keep breathing! Slow deep breaths.
9) Compare against your current income – and stay happy, regardless of what you see.
10) See where you would like to make changes and write them down.
11) Set one goal that would make a positive difference to your life.
12) Take one baby step towards your goal today.
13) Repeat step twelve tomorrow.
14) Congratulate yourself on doing this!

22. Getting Over your past

There were times
my pants were
so thin I could sit
on a dime and tell
if it was

heads or tails.

Spencer Tracy

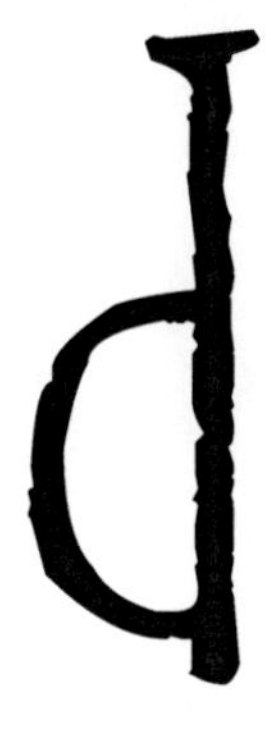

o you get annoyed by people who complain about what they can't do due to their past? Do any of these sound familiar?

- I can't run well, my teacher always told me I couldn't and I just got that in my head.
- I can't do business because I am more the Artistic type, they told me.
- When my teacher said I was stupid I believed it so I never achieved.
- I can't make much money, nobody in my family ever has.
- Ever since my mum said I was useless I feel dumb when I get stuck and I just give up.
- I can't be successful because I wasn't brought up that way.

Yes, yes, we get it, something happened and now it's still holding you back ten years, twenty years down the line. GET OVER IT.

They told Elvis Presley he couldn't sing and Marlon Brando wasn't accepted into acting school. I was told I wouldn't dance again after twisting my ankle badly but two years later I travelled the world doing just that. Christopher Reeve (the original Superman actor) fell off a horse in 1995 and was completely paralysed from the neck down and doctors said that he would never move again. His brain wouldn't accept commands any more but, with the help of electrical stimulation, Reeve engaged on a demanding exercise programme and five years later regained movement! He may not have been fully cured but he did the impossible, which also opened up a new road for research.

Why do we hold on to our past? Isn't this just silly? The following story illustrates this beautifully.

Once upon a time there were two monks walking to a village when they came to a river. A young woman who couldn't swim asked for their help so the older monk lifted her into his arms and carried her through to the other side. The two monks continued their journey but, after about an hour, the younger one clears his throat and asks, "Brother, why did you carry the woman through the river when you know we are not allowed to look at women, let alone touch them?" "Well," replies the older monk, "I carried her for a few minutes and set her down on the other side of the river, but you have been carrying her for the last hour!"

When we carry our past into our present we essentially limit ourselves. Many of us will take our memories and transfer them to the present and future. As a result we more or less replicate the past. It's a poor strategy that does not create exciting outcomes. As creative minded people, wouldn't you agree we can do much better than that?

Are you ready to reinvent the future?

When it comes to money, we want to reinvent and liberate the way we think about it, the way we deal with it. Urgently. So we have to let go of the past. We may also need to let go of our idea of the future. Because the future doesn't actually exist except in the way you think about it.

"If you want to be miserable, get yourself a future," says Byron Katie.

It is out of that present that our future is shaped[12].

12 More on that in *The Power of Now* by Eckhart Tolle.

Therefore we really want to get to grips with being in the present and living creatively in the moments that we actually have.

What does that mean? Well, for starters we may want to let go of expectations and beliefs that weigh us down.

There are a lot of teachings on the subject of letting go but it can really be explained in the simplest way: drop it[13]. Just as you can let a pen drop that you clenched in your fist. You relax the fist, turn your hand so the pen can fall down and open your hand. You can do that with any belief and view that holds you back: relax your mind, allow yourself to be open and drop the belief. There are plenty of other beliefs out there that can use some of your precious life energy.

Step one is to find out what this past consists of. My favourite exercise is the Brain Drain that we looked at in Chapter 19. I sat down and wrote everything I could think of that money meant to me. I didn't stop until everything was out. If you haven't done it yet, would you like to set some time aside for that? It's probably more effective than reading on. So getting over your past means to drop the stuff that holds you in it. One way is to examine the beliefs that may weigh you down and actively drop what needs to be dropped. Another big way we keep ourselves trapped in the past is through grudges. It's not always so easy to drop a grudge or injustice done to us or someone we love. That's where the principle of forgiveness comes in and has proven to work wonders. Forgiving is not forgetting, forgiving is the gift you give to yourself in order to release yourself from the bonds of negative emotions that keep you down (and not

---

13 This is taken from the Sedona Method. See *'The Sedona Method'* by Hale Dwoskin.

– as we tend to hope – the other person). It's a subject that deserves greater attention than this book can give it[14].

What I want to get across here is that the past is the past and the future doesn't exist yet. If we're to make one up, let's think about a good one and be very aware that we don't know how things will turn out. When it comes to money and our freedom this is important because most money stresses and worries are based on what the future may bring. And all money successes are based on what we set up and how we go about things today. The point is we have more possibilities available to us than the filters of our past experience would allow us to see. The future has not been written yet and it's yours to co-create.

At the end of the day all we have is now. Actually, we only have 'now' at the beginning of the day or in the middle of the day, and even all through the night when we don't think about it.

14 For further reading: Marci Shimoff *Happy For No Reason* and check out the work of Byron Katie.

23. if i WAS Rich

I Wouldn't Have To Worry

There are
people who have
money and
people who are

Rich

Coco Chanel

There you have the reason why many people want to be rich: so as not to worry about spending money. "I wouldn't have to think about every pound I spent – I could just buy the things I wanted." I've heard this hundreds of times, not even counting my own voice, but it is simply not true. If you were rich you'd still worry. How do I know? It's in the nature of the worried mind to find a reason to worry. If it's not about affording an H&M outfit, it will be about a shirt you saw at a designer store, a house or a holiday, attending a workshop or not, or worrying about your health, someone else's health and happiness. Or it could be work, politics, crime rates, your spouse, your lack of spouse, why there are no good men/women in the world or why there are too many good men/women in the world. You'll always find something. If you didn't have to worry about money, you'd worry whether your friends love you for you or for your cash, whether new acquaintances are genuine or not. You are creative; you'll come up with something!

Artrepreneur Principle 17:

Worry is worry no matter how much money you have.

If not having to worry is what you are after, you can have it now. Worry does not equal care even if people like me may have confused one with the other. You can care about making more money and you can care about the environment without worrying. The more you really care, the less you will want to waste your energy with worry.

The most common worry about stopping to worry is that for some reason we'd stop taking action. Well, you might be conditioned to frighten yourself into taking action – "work hard or you'll never get anywhere!" – but it doesn't have to be that way. In fact it's dangerously unproductive in the long run. Worry causes stress and stress is the number one trigger of illnesses these days – and the number one killer! Have you noticed that worry is hard work and nobody pays you for it?

We can motivate ourselves in different ways:

1) Through pain and fear including (self-proclaimed or imagined) threats about what will happen if you don't do this or that (I'd better get paid work fast or I'll be on the street!) worries and "shoulding" all over yourself (Oh, I really should keep my books neat). It stinks.
2) Motivation can also be sourced from love and conscious choice. Which is very powerful and cool. There is research proving it but I don't think we need that here. You know the truth.

To tackle my worried relationship with money, I once engaged in a daring challenge where I walked around with £1,000 cash for one month. The idea was to take all your money and walk around with it for a month. I took £1,000 as that was a highly uncomfortable, unnerving, exciting amount at the time and bore enough risk for me to 'feel' the game yet wouldn't leave me homeless (just yet) should something happen. It would have been a real issue losing it, though. Don't get me wrong, it was A LOT for me. Entrepreneurial speaker and trainer Daniel Priestly suggested this exercise and shared with us how he learned from this - he had done it with £3,000. When you walk around with your money in cash, you realise that you can actually afford more than you thought you could. I walked into shops and looked at clothes labelled £200 and up. Normally I would just walk past because it's way above my budget. But in this month I realised, well, I have £1,000 on me right now, I could actually buy this, but I simply chose not to and I started feeling rich. I stopped being the 'poor struggling artist' and grew into a more mature money consciousness. "I have money."

Running around with £1,000 in cash was unnerving. Picking it up at the bank had me feeling like a criminal: asking for £1,000 in cash and then sitting there while they counted it made me blush and I felt embarrassed. Could there be so much emotional attachment to these pieces of paper? I'd think people could sense I had the money and would attack me for it. It's really interesting to observe your thoughts. "Oh, gosh, will someone mug me? I am such a good target right now. Would people suspect I have £1,000 on me?" At night I'd drive myself even more insane thinking non-stop about how much money I had on me. After a while I stopped bothering so much. It became normal: yes, I have £1,000 on me, so what? I could buy everyone in the pub a round if I wanted. I can get home in a cab. I certainly don't need a cash machine. I could walk around comfortably being me. I relaxed with the money and I even did a performance with the money belt on. Nobody in the audience knew that the little Madonna impersonator on stage was loaded with a grand tucked away in her fishnets. It felt daring and slutty.

How can we expect ourselves to be relaxed around money when it makes us so nervous to have it?

If you want to play it, take as much cash as you can to feel uncomfortable enough and carry it with you everywhere. In your wallet, bra, money belt, wherever, and if you spend or lose some of it or all of it, you must replace it. I feel a little uncomfortable recommending this game because it feels so risky, if you don't have so much and you lose it all, so please play this game responsibly at your own risk.

But to be honest with you, I benefited hugely myself from playing it. Thinking about what you can lose keeps you small and playing safe. There is nothing wrong with thinking about safety but growth is not always safe. Life isn't always safe. We didn't come here to go safely to our death. And if you lose your cash for any reason, you will realise even more so, that money is a renewable energy.

24. Feeling Rich

Is A State Of Mind. Give Me A VISA!

Money, it turned out, was exactly like sex, you thought of nothing else if you didn't have it and thought of other things

if you did.

James Arthur Baldwin

24. Feeling Rich Is A State Of Mind. Give Me A VISA!

s we have already explored, you could have plenty of money and feel impoverished, always needing more. Who knows how long the money will last? But not having much in your bank doesn't mean you have to feel poor. Feeling rich is therefore not a numbers game but a state of mind. It's the extent to which you enjoy what you have.

Let's get practical: say you want to buy organic food and for you it is really expensive so you will need to budget. Write down exactly how much you have to spend and spend accordingly – in other words that's living within your means. You might not have a lot of cash but don't let that affect your *feeling* of wealth. Don't let anyone take your wealth confidence.

So how do we access this state? Is there a border to cross and a passport to show?

Yes, there is border control: the way you relate to money and your choices will decide if you can come into the land of feeling wealthy or not. We once played a game at a seminar that left most people deeply confused but I was one of the few winners, so I liked the game: the idea was that we were put into an ever-changing market; we all had a few resources that were given to us and the goal was to get into the circle at the front. That was the winners' circle, but you were only allowed in by the gate-keepers. The rules didn't become clearer over the game, things were changing and people were getting really upset. In that sense, this game was just like real life. We all wanted to get into this circle but how to crack the code? Was it who had got the most ropes (our currency in the game) or was it about who had the most friends or who manipulated the gate-keepers? Was it about determination? Was it about ambition?

The goal wasn't to win, or to get the most 'money' or 'ropes' but it was to be at peace with the fact that it's a game. Now that outcome is really useful for real life. Being at peace with the fact that money and business is a game we all play: a game with changing rules where things don't always make sense. Not everything is fair.

Can you be at peace with that? That's the visa to the land of feeling rich.

25. How Wealthy Are You, Really?

Every day I get up and look through the Forbes list of the richest people in America. If I'm not there, I

go to work.

Robert Orben

Feeling poor is a feeling of being limited: I can't afford this food. I can't afford this holiday; I can't afford to work with this coach. It's a focus on all that you cannot have right now.

Feeling poor is being stuck in your limitations.

Feeling rich is the feeling of freedom, of having all or more than you need, and of being at peace with the game.

If you want to feel rich, how about you refocus on what you DO have and build it from there? If you are up for it, start by counting all the things you have and appreciate in your life. Just to bring this fact back home: simply by having been born in the northern hemisphere we are already amongst the 20% of the richest people on this planet. Whether you feel it or not, it's a fact. That's a pretty good head start, isn't it? You can read, write, you have an education and a roof over your head. Even if you don't do any more, you'll always be kind of all right just because of where you live. That's the sort of wealth we have here and you get to be a part of it simply because you've been born here – it's quite incredible.

So most of us are dealing with luxury problems of how to get more and how to fulfil more of our dreams. We may think that as Artistic Souls we are at a disadvantage in comparison to the money makers of our society. Everyone is great at comparing themselves to those who have more, but how little we compare ourselves to those who have less – although there are many more who have less! Sometimes it's good to bear in mind how well we are doing in the great scheme of things.

I remember an American client stressing out about money, as she was terrified of losing her house and ending up on the street. They have no welfare system. She felt threatened so felt she mustn't spend a penny! But what would happen if she lost her house? Would she really be living on the streets? No. She'd be with family or friends until she'd get a smaller apartment or room somewhere. That's how rich we are. I'm not saying people in the Northern hemisphere don't ever struggle to make ends meet but, as anyone who has travelled the world will confirm, even if you have 'nothing' here you still have many more resources and more support than impoverished people living in places like India, Africa and South America for example.

Another way to look at being rich is not to define it by how much you have right now but at how fast you could recreate your wealth if it was taken from you. It occurred to me on my travels that even if I lost everything, I wouldn't end up on the street for the rest of my life. I would always find my way around and rebuild my life. That made me feel really good and secure. Making money is not just about where you've been born. There are plenty of self-made millionaires that came from humble backgrounds to prove that. If Richard Branson woke up in your life, in your body, how long do you think it would take him to rebuild his fortune? He'd do it quite fast – much faster than you and I would – because he is incredibly skilled at making money and creating businesses. What this shows is:

ARtREPRENEUR PRINCIPLE 18:

Making money is a skill, not a coincidence.

And skills are learnt. It all starts by developing your interest and getting stuck in. We need entrepreneurial education. Not necessarily official schooling. Academic education in itself isn't the key – remember that having a PhD doesn't necessarily mean you make good money. We need more understanding of how things work. Educate our minds about how to ask for money, how to keep track of it, what to spend on and invest in, who to do business with, how to recognise the pitfalls.

These days education is readily available and, thanks to the Internet, a lot of it is free, and now books are cheaper than ever. Although investing in education always pays great returns, if you invest your money into your own money development then you will end up with more in your wallet over time.

So how rich are you actually?

I remember realising how rich I was when I found myself in jail in Guatemala (long story for the next book) when, out of a group of eight, four of us got arrested and the other four brought us food, blankets and sweets. We were in a small cage under the staircase of the police station and the bars looked onto the plaza of the small mountain village. Children who stank of pee and looked hungry slowly walked up to us. We ended up feeding them from inside the bars – sharing our candy and other goodies with them. How bizarre is that? We were locked up and we still had more food than they did because we had more access to resources. So that's one way of finding out how rich you really are: look at how much access you have to resources. It's not just your own physical wealth that determines what you can move and shake in the world but whose networks and wealth you have access to. How much money and other resources do your friends have? What have you got access to that other people don't? It can be anything from fresh water to holiday homes.

Another way to discover how rich you already are in the sense of real numbers is to look at the amount of time you could live without working and getting any more money in. How many days/weeks/months/years could you go on before you'd really land on the street? Even when I felt super poor, I had about four months I could have survived without doing anything. Now that is quite a long time – in four months you can do a lot including finding a job – but I acted and lived as if my very existence would be threatened by my poverty. That's not just because I am a little dramatic at times – it's because I didn't see this clearly.

What's the point in feeling poor? It doesn't pay the rent. It's not creative.

26. I WANT IT ALL.

Now!

If you can count your money, you don't have a

billion dollars.

J. Paul Getty

This is a question I received from Zeth in Denmark:

> *Is it possible for me to ever feel rich? I mean, a creative mind can have so many ideas on what to do, how to invest, what to buy, where to go on holiday, when to take a holiday, where to spend the weekend, how to decorate your living room, what to wear etc. I have what I need: a laptop, a phone, clothes to wear – but I mean rich rich. So rich that I don't have to consider if I can afford the organic food in the supermarket. Where, when I get a new idea, I can just go ahead and do it without thinking about my bank account. Is it a state of mind – a spending-approach to everything? Or is it my creative mind that keeps pumping ideas through the roof that I want to do? So here's my question – can I become financially free without giving up dreams and ideas?*

The answer is YES, OF COURSE! In fact you can only become free if you keep up the dreams and ideas. Here is the Artistic Soul's dilemma; we have a hundred ideas and only twenty-four hours in the day and not necessarily much in our bank account to do anything about it. Will this ever change? No. As humans, we are naturally restricted. We can widen the restrictions – when I was twenty-four I felt my financial circumstances were paralysing me as I couldn't afford even the train ticket to London to get myself onto the open mic stages in order to work my way up. All I wanted was to move in the world. Enough money to do what I needed to do in order to get on with it!

But even when I had the money for the train tickets, something else was missing: the time, or the energy, or the new comedy material, or simply my desire to go. When life becomes a game of chasing what we don't have, it gets really uncomfortable. At least Artistic Souls tend to take the scenic route to the land of burnout. But it's still burnout.

The point in life is not to do everything that comes into your mind but to find what you actually want. So finding out what you really, really want is a great way to lead a much more satisfying and productive life. How do you do that? You hire a coach, talk to a friend or use this incredibly simple tool.

SECRET TOOL TO FIND OUT WHAT YOU REALLY WANT:

What would ***insert what you think you want*** give me? Keep asking this until you have drilled down to the real desire behind the want.

Now Zeth doesn't just want to know if he'll ever be free, he wants to know how he can do all the wonderful things that inspire him, how he can make his ideas a reality. So here is a note on how the creative process – making things that didn't exist before exist – happens.

The creative process has three phases, named by Robert Fritz as germination, assimilation and completion. I would like to rename them to these three stages: collecting, developing, completing[15].

---

15 To read more about Robert Fritz's theory on the creative process, see his book *The Path Of Least Resistance*.

Stage 1 – Collecting means we dream up ideas, possibly lots. To proceed to the next stage we need to decide on which one we want to make into a reality.

Stage 2 – Developing is when you start working on the idea, actually doing something about it. You keep going and going until you decide that it's time for the final stage.

Stage 3 – Completing is the place where many of us like to get stuck because whatever we created, the song, the invention, the theatre piece... it's still not PERFECT. Or by now we have many more ideas on how to make it better; we want to keep working on it. In order to create something useful, we must complete and then release our creation into the world.

Why was this important to note? Because when we don't understand these three stages, we tend to get very distracted by ideas popping into our heads when we least need them. We may stop work on perfectly good projects to court the latest idea. We fall in love with a younger model. The question is therefore not only will I ever have enough money to make all my ideas happen but also: how do I make powerful, satisfying choices?

To have what we want, we choose what we really, really want first and commit to creating that.

As a practical tool I strongly recommend using an ideas book or using a folder on your computer called ideas. This way, incoming ideas get noted down there and reviewed later and you don't have to worry about missing out on the big idea, plus you will not be controlled by all the thoughts coming into your head. Just put them down and then close the book/file. Your idea is safe and will be there for you when you are ready.

How to find out what you really really really want for NOW exercise:

1) *Start writing a list of all the things you want to have, be and do in your life.* This will probably be a long and colourful list at first. You can even make a mind map, which is easier for a lot of visual people. There are great mind mapping software programs you can find through Google, or take out your pen and paper and get going.

2) *Take another sheet and draw up a timeline starting now, going up to the next ten years.* Now go ahead and drop your desires into a time frame. For example: owning my own house would be in the next ten years, but buying my first flat in two. Going skiing could be in the next five years, so I make a little marker on the year and write 'going skiing'. You can add financial goals into this too, but remember it's more meaningful to imagine the things you'll do and experience than to drop in random numbers.

   When you do this, you will already begin to feel some of the desires to be more urgent and stronger than others. You will gain the clarity that not all ideas and wishes occupy the same space. Where the cluster of ideas clouded your clear thinking, you will find space and clarity. This example shows how I did it:

1 year from now	2 years	3 years	4 years	5 years
Baby	Wedding?	2nd baby		
Study	Master's degree			
	Buy a flat			Buy house
	Children's album	Adult music album	Children's book	My own show?
Great private practice	Madly sought after coach and speaker			
Workshops	Retreat and workshop			

3) Make a note of those things that are really important to you.

4) Then collate a list of goals that are the most important.

5) Ask yourself: which one of these, if I dedicated my time and energy to it now, will have the biggest impact, make the biggest difference in my life?

That is what you really, really want for now.

27. Financial

Freedom

It is pretty
hard to tell
what does bring

HAPPINESS;

poverty and
wealth have both
failed.

Kin Hubbard

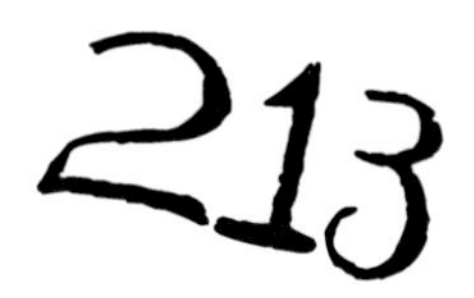

There are two ways of defining financial freedom:

1) The amount of money you need in order not to lift a finger and cover all your living costs.
2) The feeling of being free when it comes to money and your finances.

Having enough money to cover all your living expenses without lifting a finger and feeling free are two different things. It is tempting to think, "When I have the money, I will have the feeling, too," but enough millionaires have been observed and studied for us to understand they don't necessarily feel free[16].

The more money you get, the more responsibilities you have; there are always challenges or problems and as your income goes up so do your expenses. Rich people have big lifestyles to maintain so the gap between what they have and what they need can easily squeeze them, too. Many a rich (wo)man has gone from 'having a lot' to 'everything has gone to pot' as missing out on the same level of income can take you down the drain very quickly. So just having a million – or whatever your dream number at the moment is – is still not the solution to a wealthy and abundant life!

In order to really gain financial freedom you need to master the four pillars of money and that means understanding how to acquire it, spend it, invest it and

16 See Sonja Lyubormirsky, *The How of Happiness*; Paul McKenna, *I Can Make You Rich*; Robert Holden, *Success Intelligence,* p.117; Michael Neill, *Feel Happy Now*.

keep it – though not necessarily in that order. If money is important to you, and I hope this book inspires you this way, please go forth and learn more about it! As a singer I studied over ten years to develop my voice and skills. As a coach I've been studying over a decade and it's just the beginning. Whatever your expertise, you will have spent time on it so how can you expect to be great at money when you have never spent any energy learning about it? You can cultivate financial freedom without a million in the bank. Remember that the Be-Do-Have model suggests it's easier for us to make the money when we already feel the freedom. But it is not a requirement: you can stay stressed and worried about money and still make more. You just won't enjoy it much and chances are the money goes out faster than it came in. Studies show that lottery winners tend to eventually go back to the same financial level they were at before their win.

If you are not prepared for money in your life, it will flow out like a breeze through your open window.

Paul McKenna talks about a wealth thermostat: the idea that we are used to a certain amount of money and that somehow we maintain that. Psychologists speak about set points. When we make more, we somehow 'lose' it again and when we have less we work harder to reach our comfort level. The idea is that we need to change the level on our thermostat first to allow ourselves to be comfortable with more. Where is your thermostat set at the moment? Are you willing to turn it up and by how much? Where is your 'eek-uncomfortable' point? Think yourself up to the number at which you feel

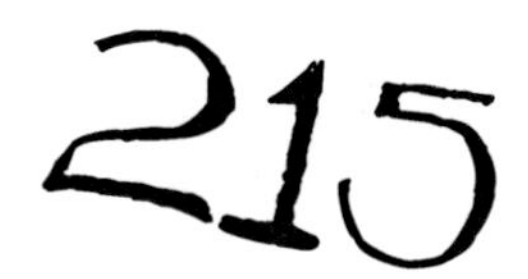

uncomfortable. For example: would you be happy to make £100,000 a year or £200,000, £500,000 - even £1,000,000? When do you start feeling strange/wrong about it/don't buy into the possibility of it?

Now, let's have a look at the number that would have you being financially independent. Where you didn't have to work any more and covered all your living costs. Some people need £300,000, others £10 million to achieve their financial independence. Feel cosmopolitan and think in your own currency if you wish.

So where are you? Would you like to find out what you would need to be completely financially independent?

The Financial Independence Day exercise

Step 1: Write down the living expenses of the lifestyle you want to have and that is the money you need to generate every year.

Example:

I want to live in a beautiful house in London that costs around £1 million.

Let's say the mortgage for that is £3,000 a month. (I probably paid a big chunk up front to get a mortgage like that.)

I spend £500 on wonderful food.

I go to the theatre once a week. Good seats, darling, £50 x4 = £200.

I spend £2,000 on living expenses.

I give £200 as charity donations.

I save £500 each month for holidays.

I spend £500 each month on family days.
That makes a total of: £6,900 per month. Let's round that up to £7,000 a month.
£7000 x 12 = £84,000 a year (after tax!)

When I did this exercise we were told that you can make 8% interest on average if you choose wise investments, but that seems like a really dated idea, it's more likely to be 4% max. However, these things change and I'll play with 4% in this example.

One way of finding your financial independence number is to assume that you can get 4% interest from an asset and therefore if you multiply your number by 25 you will have the amount you'd need to have in the bank[17]. That number gives us a good indication of what we are actually talking about when we say financially free. I'm only talking about a couple of million, not ten or more, but if you count all my dreams together and see what they cost in total, they come to four million. But with only two million I could easily create a wonderful dream lifestyle allowing for everything in time without doing anything. I don't even need a million to be

---

17 For those of you who wish to know how I calculated the multiplier of 25, here we go;
I want to know how much I need invested at 4% that will give me an income of £84,000.
So, what is the number of which 4% is 84,000?
First, 4% is the same as the decimal number 0.04.
I took the 84,000 (yearly cost) and divided it by 0.04. That gives me the number that 84k is 4% of.
The number you will find from your calculator is 2,100,000.
and 84,000 divided by 2,100,000 is 25.
Alternatively, how many 4%s are there in 100%? Answer, 25.
Multiply 84,000 by 25.

super happy and wealthy because if you know how to play with your money so that it makes you some more – and allows you to spend it with wisdom and fun – then you are sorted, mate!

Again, this isn't a substitute for professional financial advice but it showed me where my dreams were at. Before this exercise I had no clue what I'd be looking at to be 'rich' or 'living the dream financially'. Note the dream changes and so do the numbers, so this is about learning how to do this rather than staying fixed on one number for the rest of your life. After all, you update your portfolio, your business cards – so we also need to keep updating the numbers on our dreams.

Now let's talk about your dreams: do you know what all of them added together would cost? Most of us run around thinking 'too much' and 'it would never happen' without actually knowing what the 'it' number is. Madness. So let's shed some light here, too.

Exercise:

Create a mind map of your dreams, from travelling the world to the five-star holidays in Mauritius to your dream villa or whatever it is to you. You could just make a list, though you may find that a mind map makes it easier to go from one to the next easily.

Then transfer the results into a spreadsheet to research the costs involved. Whatever sounds like more fun, and tickles all your dreams out of you, do it. When you have researched how much you need to pay for those dreams, add it all together. Here is an excerpt from one of my spreadsheets, just to give

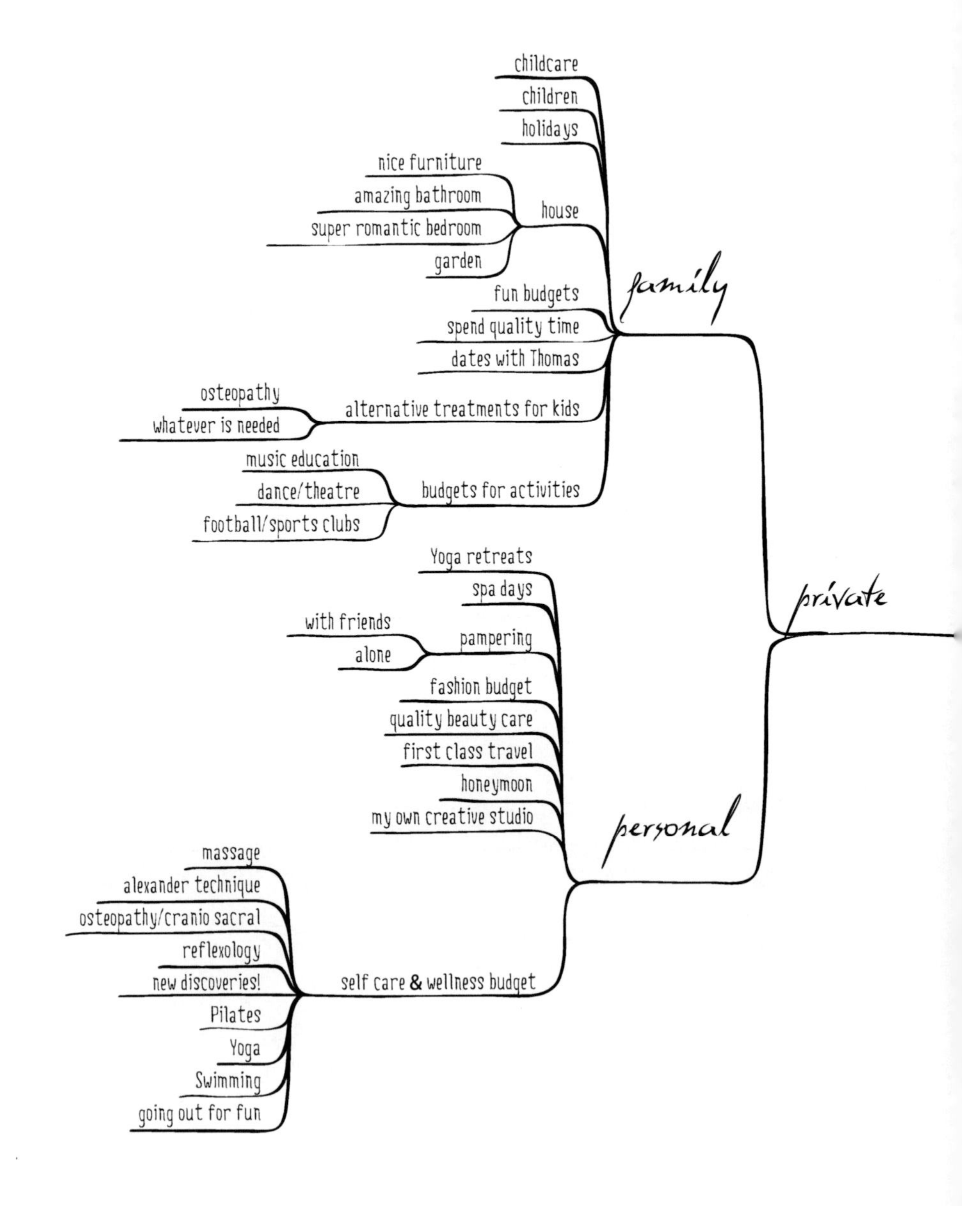
childcare
children
holidays
nice furniture
amazing bathroom
super romantic bedroom
garden
house
fun budgets
spend quality time
dates with Thomas
osteopathy
whatever is needed
alternative treatments for kids
music education
dance/theatre
football/sports clubs
budgets for activities
family
private
Yoga retreats
spa days
with friends
alone
pampering
fashion budget
quality beauty care
first class travel
honeymoon
my own creative studio
personal
massage
alexander technique
osteopathy/cranio sacral
reflexology
new discoveries!
Pilates
Yoga
Swimming
going out for fun
self care & wellness budget

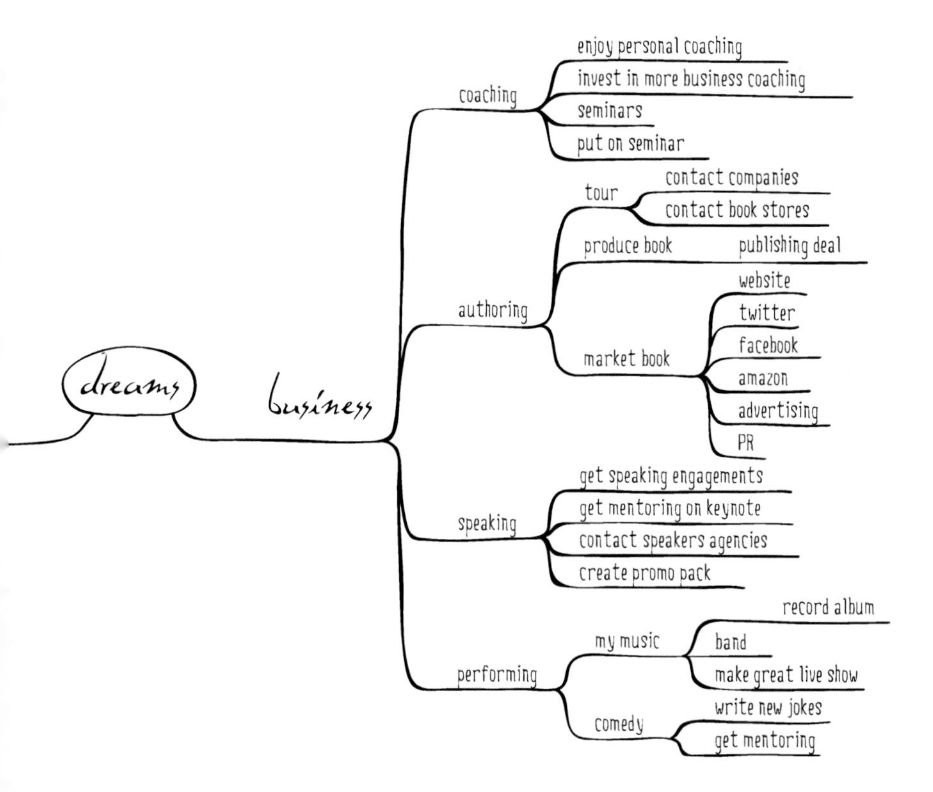
dreams
business
coaching
enjoy personal coaching
invest in more business coaching
seminars
put on seminar
authoring
tour
contact companies
contact book stores
produce book
publishing deal
market book
website
twitter
facebook
amazon
advertising
PR
speaking
get speaking engagements
get mentoring on keynote
contact speakers agencies
create promo pack
performing
my music
record album
band
make great live show
comedy
write new jokes
get mentoring

you an idea, and thank you to my friend CB for coming up with it in the first place. The South America Travel you see on here probably would have never happened had we not calculated the costs about a year and a half earlier. But as I knew what I needed I could prepare. Sure, it took another eighteen months to actually happen but that's relatively quick compared to the four years talking and dreaming about it.

Dream Venture	Units	People involved	Price per unit	Total Price
South America travel				
Tour	1	2	£1200	£2400
Flight	1	2	£900	£1800
Hotel	5	2	£80	£800
Food	60	2	£15	£1800
Travel expenses	60	2	£10	£1200
Activities	30	2	£10	£600
Africa travel				£0
Working with lions	1	2	£1,800	£3600
Flight working with lions	1	2	£700	£1400
Safari	1	2	£700	£1400
				£0
US travel				£0
Flight	1	2	£700	£1400
Car hire	60	1	£50	£3000
Hotel	60	1	£80	£4800

Dream Venture	Units	People involved	Price per unit	Total Price
Food	60	2	£30	£3600
Activities	20	2	£25	£1000

It's fascinating what happens when you start looking into your dreams and ideas. Some of them you'll already feel at that stage aren't quite as exciting as they were in your head, and others start becoming very prominent.

28. do you Deserve To Be Rich?

empty pockets

never held
anyone back.
Only empty
heads and empty
hearts can do
that.

Norman Vincent Peale

I still remember that day in elementary school. We finished our swimming class and huddled together in the tram taking us back to the main school building across town. It was a cold day; my hair was still wet. Having rushed to catch up with the rest of the class, I was standing close to my teacher, Miss King, whom I remember fondly. I took out my home-made cheese sandwich on my favourite German rye bread and took a hearty bite, saying "Boah, das hab ich mir wirklich verdient" – which is German for "I really deserve this. I have really earned this one". Miss King looked at me with that sharp and kind expression of hers and corrected me: "No, you haven't."

I didn't dare to ask her what she meant. I felt too embarrassed, and for years I couldn't solve this riddle. She hadn't said it in a nasty way. I hadn't done anything wrong. I had swum my little heart out, I was there, I was hungry, and why didn't I deserve this? I had totally earned my right to eat after all that effort. You should have seen me swim! Did she mean I hadn't actually worked in exchange for the sandwich? Or that other people would deserve it more? Was I being a spoilt brat for considering myself as having earned this sandwich when all I had done was swim where other people worked in the fields? I really didn't get it. Was she just being mean and condescending?

It's only now that I work with people and their need for deserving that I realise why she said this. Eating and enjoying your sandwich has nothing to do with deserving or earning it. I was hungry and I had a sandwich. I ate it and I enjoyed it. Someone else might have worked even harder and be hungry and not have a sandwich. I had the sandwich independently of my hard work. My work didn't earn me the right to eat it. I could have sat in class all day and still had the sandwich.

When it comes to money I have the pleasure of liberating people from their belief that they have to earn their place in the world, that they deserve what they get. We probably developed this belief from our religious and cultural backgrounds. Making people feel inadequate about what they have is a great way of controlling them. Guilt and shame are such effective control mechanisms. Very clever people in power knew how to keep their power, and some of the residue of that is still floating around. We don't really deserve anything in the positive or negative sense of the word. Factory workers probably work much harder than a lawyer sitting in a nice warm office with a cup of coffee and yet the lawyer makes much more money. It's not about deserving. Life doesn't work like that. Some of us are blessed with a good start in life, others with more challenges.

It's not the cards we've been handed that determine whether we do well in this game. It's how we play them.

Some Artistic Souls I have met find it hard to make money because they feel ashamed to ask for it. They feel they'd be taking something away from someone else and that would be wrong. They want the world to be fair, they can't stand the injustice and they don't want to hurt anyone. Shame and embarrassment are the other side of the deserving coin. Lucy, for example, would say: "Surely if I make too much money, someone else will not have enough. I want to be affordable to those who really need me and they don't have much money!"

I asked Lucy if I sent her to go to the supermarket to get ten bags of apples, would she have an issue with it? No, she wouldn't. It turns out she really likes apples so I point out that if she buys ten bags of apples, there will be ten bags less for other people to get.

"Oh, but they'll get more tomorrow," says Lucy. Sure, I'll say, but apples are a limited resource. What if someone else wants to juice over the weekend or make apple pie and has been looking forward to it for a long time? They only grow at certain times and if we eat more than there are, then there will be a shortage.

But Lucy will not see the problem as dramatic. She is way too convinced about the fact that there are enough apples for everyone (whether that is actually true or not, that's how she perceives it). I asked her if she could see money as apples, how would she feel about it?

"Oh, but it's only apples we are talking about."

Yes, and it's only money. Each day, we are confronted with the suggestion that money is powerful, that it demands our attention and submission. One of the oldest scripture classics – the bible – talks about not worshipping the golden calf. The way I understand it is that material things – including money – are deceivingly tempting to worship. It's easy to surrender our mental, physical and emotional energy to them. But money is not (a) god. It's not alive. It's just a symbol; just like the golden calf wasn't ever going to be a real cow. A real cow is useful but a symbol merely has an agreed value. If you take a golden cow to Mars, they will not know what to do with it unless they eat gold there or use it to feed their pigs with – in which case they'd like it. My personal guess is they would want to trade in giraffes.

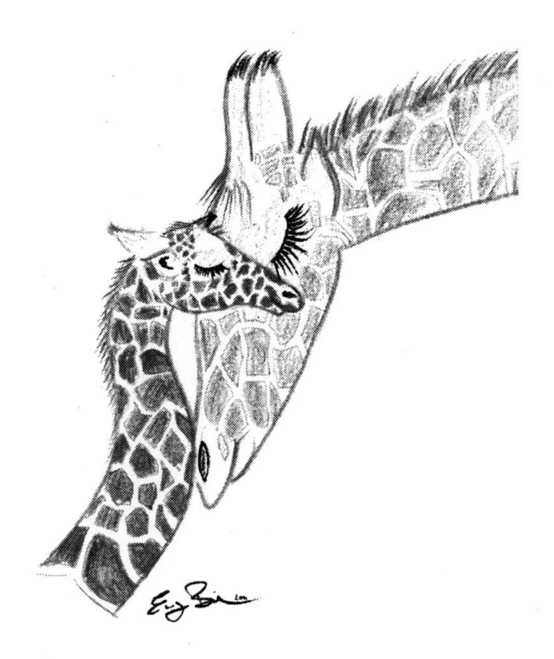

The point from which we successfully strayed was: Money is only money and not something to surrender our divine spirit to.

When we free our mind from making money the number one focus of our energy, and instead direct it to our true values, our spiritual values, our heart, we lead much more peaceful and abundant lives.

The other question is: are you allowing yourself to be rich?

Is it okay for *you* to make lots of money? Or will you only accept a certain level of income because any more would be more than you deserve. Especially when receiving vast amounts for what was fun such as a book, a film, artwork, it

can feel a bit intimidating: but I didn't work *that* hard for it. I've done so many other things that aren't paid. Am I worth that much? You may have met people who did not feel worthy of the wealth that was bestowed upon them. The consequence: they either get rid of the money quickly or they feel really bad about having it. Usually the two go hand-in-hand. They might not be the most conscious of actions. I for one haven't met anyone saying in words: I feel so bad about having more money than I feel I am worth, I am going to let go of it as fast as I can in the most useless ways possible.

Actions speak louder than words.

Just check in with yourself: how much money would you be okay with receiving? Would it be okay to be paid £10,000 for your work? Would it be okay to be paid £20,000? £50,000? £100,000? £1,000,000?

When I first heard about this I thought – I can take being paid shit loads! Bring it on, people, I'll deal with the issue if it arises. Bring on the cash, I'll pay the therapist later if needed.

But in a quiet moment I found that there was indeed a number at which I felt uncomfortable. Being paid £10,000 for a performance, for example, felt like a very different kind of pressure than £500.

How much do you need to make a year before you go, "Okay, okay, stop. This is getting really freaky"?

Self-worth is a buzzword in the self development world. Not feeling worthy is a real biggie for many. Actually I doubt there is anyone who has never felt the "am I really worth that?" doubt.

And yet one cannot put a monetary worth on the life of a human being. Okay, one can (and it has been done frequently throughout history), but it will never be right. How can one life be worth more than another?

'Worth' and 'wealth' are quite similar words. And in economic terms we speak of people being worth $1 billion based on their wealth. But that's not really the worth of the person. It's the economic worth of that person as a business entity. Self-worth in contrast relates to the idea that you can value yourself. You can value yourself financially (how much money you have produced) and you can value yourself in terms of how much you actually accept and appreciate yourself. And it is interesting how we use the word value for both: what I hold important, i.e. what I value and how much is this worth? – what's the value?

If you don't like yourself, how do you expect to take great care of yourself? Why would you? What for? And do you really think you'd like yourself more if you had more money? Since when is self-love bought?

So that's another way of getting in our own way. Expecting to do well in life when I don't like myself very much is a really mean game. If I succeed, doing well in life feels bad because I don't like myself. I'm miserable by default, or at least silently unhappy. It's easy to associate the self depreciation with the results it seems to have produced (in the case of worldly success). And that's where it gets twisted – this is where artists feel the (unconscious) need to keep the suffering up, often by creating highly dramatic private lives, for example, as that seems to produce the hit songs. Amy Winehouse springs to mind here, as well as Edith Piaf and many more revered experts in self-loathing.

And if I don't get to do well in life and I don't like myself, I've got even more reasons to beat myself up about it.

There is NO win.

If I was your Psychology columnist in your favourite magazine I'd write: you need to start loving yourself. You must value yourself. You need to work on your self-esteem and your self-worth. I'd make sure I put all those words in to make me look as though I really know what you need to do.

And you'd love me for my advice and live happily ever after ignoring it as we do with most advice, especially if we read it in a psychology magazine.

There is a joke saying psychology solves problems we never knew we had in the first place[18].

My take is that self-worth is one of those problems that we only have when we believe in the concept. If you didn't know or buy into the idea that a human could be worth more or less, you couldn't feel worthless.

If only you knew that you are love, and divine and a miracle. If only you knew that you are pure potential and you are energy free to create... If only you knew how powerful you are. If you could really take that in for a minute. An hour. A lifetime. Thank you.

There is NO amount of money that can make up for you being on earth. This being here is really all we've got right now. And that's a whole lot more than our rational minds are able to grasp. Ask anyone who has ever lost a loved one. Ask anyone who has ever been close to death. That's when we get reminded. Or now.

So if no amount of money can equate to us being here, let's just get very clear that the money people pay us is not money they pay us as humans or for being a person. It's

18 I do not recollect the originator of this joke but if you know the author or are the author, please get in touch and I shall credit you and admire you personally for your wit.

money we collect for a service, a product, a brand we created. Sometimes it's money for our time invested. But it cannot pay me as a human. It can only be a token. Even the Million.

You absolutely deserve it. ☺

29. Instant Wealth

What difference does it make how much you have? What you do not have amounts to much more.

Seneca

What is it about being rich that you would like? Is it the big conference table with the glass chandelier and the Rolls-Royce outside the door? What I always admired when I went to see rich people's houses was not that they had lots of stuff, in fact often they didn't have lots of stuff at all. They had fewer but select top quality items and everything looked new and sparkling. That impressed me because in my house things were mostly messy and cleaning was no one's priority. I thought that the wealthy just have nicer things, but I had to admit they must be taking care of their things too, otherwise they would get worn out just like everyone else's. Now my next thought was that they don't have to do it themselves, so they have it easy and poor little me, not only do I suffer from an overload of cheap stuff and a mess, I also have to clean. Well, I am here to report I have now witnessed that many people I would consider well-off do indeed clean their own things. It's the little things like sparkling taps in the bathroom and clean kitchen surfaces that make a difference. When I want to feel rich, one thing I can do is get down and really clean my flat.

From a law of attraction perspective taking care of your things attracts more of those things to you. So taking care of your money and what it buys you attracts more money. I'm not huge on the law of attraction, but I am a fan of the law of creation – and what we are talking about here is where pop psychology meets common sense:

What you focus on, grows.
And what you own, you are responsible for.

This is beautifully written about in the adult fairy tale *The Little Prince* by the philosopher and scientist Antoine de Saint-Exupéry. The little Prince comes from a distant planet and has fallen onto Earth; he's on an adventure, meeting other creatures to find out what life is all about. On his own planet he got bored and a little depressed being alone with his three volcanoes and a rose and the baobab seeds he has to weed out. In this scene he meets the fox.

(The Fox is hiding under a tree)
F – I'm a fox.
LP – Come and play with me.
F – I can't play with you. I'm not tamed.
LP – What does that mean, 'tame'?
F – What are you looking for?
LP – I'm looking for friends. What does that mean, 'tame'?
F – It's an act too often neglected. It means to establish ties.
LP – 'To establish ties'?
F – Just that. To you I'm nothing more than a fox like a hundred thousand other foxes. But if you tame me, then we'll need each other. To me you'll be unique in all the world. To you I'll be unique in all the world...
LP – I'm beginning to understand. There's a flower... I think that she's tamed me.
F – Please, tame me!
LP – I want to, very much, but I haven't much time. I have friends to discover, and a great many things to understand.

F – One only understands the things that one tames. Men buy things all ready made in shops. But there's no shop where you can buy friendship, and so men have no friends any more. If you want a friend, tame me.

LP – What must I do to tame you?

F – You must be very patient. First you'll sit down at a little distance from me, like that, in the grass. I'll look at you and you'll say nothing. Words are the source of misunderstandings. But you'll sit a little closer to me, every day.

LP – I think we're friends already. But now it's time for me to go.

F – Can't you stay a little longer? If you go, I'll cry!

LP – It's your own fault. I never wished you any sort of harm. You wanted me to tame you!

F – Yes, that is so. Before you go I want to tell you a secret: it's only with the heart that one can see clearly; what is essential is invisible to the eye.

LP – What is essential is invisible to the eye...

F – It's the time you've spent on your rose that makes your rose so important.

LP – It's the time I've spent on my rose...

F – Men have forgotten this truth. But you mustn't forget it! You become responsible, forever, for what you've tamed. You're responsible for your rose.

LP – I'm responsible for my rose. (The Prince repeats the Fox's words and sets out on his journey.)

I am responsible for my rose, my new shower gel, my clothes. To me this thought has taught me to take greater care of my things. I wear this jumper; it's my responsibility to take care of it. My mum tried for years to teach me this when she found my clothes neglected on the floor, but fables work much better for this than mums. Sorry, Mum. Have you noticed yourself treating an expensive jumper better than a cheap one? What is essential is invisible to the eyes... Our relationships with our things are what make us feel rich or poor.

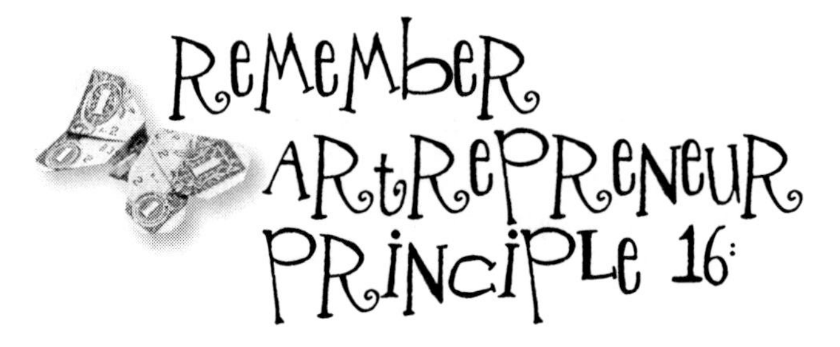

The magic of transformation lies in deep care.

My resentment towards my cheap stuff I never wanted in the first place is what made me feel poor, not the fact that I didn't have lots. This was also underlined by my wonderful flatmate Siv. She wanted to clean her slate and detach from material things to think more clearly and be freer in the world, so she sold her belongings in Norway and gave lots of her stuff away. She rented a small room in our flat in London and contented herself with the few things she had. One of my nightmares is to have to live in a small room with hardly anything but she made it her choice. I admired her endlessly for it and cherish the revelation that what I considered my doom isn't even that big a deal!

I always perceived her as wealthy. To be honest, she could have dressed in cheap clothes and she would have still come across as rich to me. It was the grace and joy with which she carried herself. In contrast another flatmate who lived in the room before her earned more money than any of us but always felt poor and looked much more scruffy. Don't get me wrong, she had a very interesting personality and was at times a wonderful friend. It was the way she was treating what she had, the way things were thrown around and how uncared for things were that determined this perception.

Many of us Artistic Souls find it hard to select just a few nice things to keep and let the rest go. Most Artistic Souls I know are also collectors, hoarders and 'just in case'-ers – often keeping things because they might come in handy one day. My mum is a specialist in that respect, and the things do come in handy sometimes. Thank you, Mum, for keeping the bubble wrap for ten years until I needed it. I still have the faded-rose coloured velvet string she put in my advent calendar around 1986 or so. It made it so special I didn't use it up and I would never throw it out because it's 'very valuable'. It did come in handy when I wrapped a present for my loved one fifteen years later. To show him how much I loved him, I used some of the special velvet string.

I wouldn't call myself a hoarder, of course not, I just keep all the things I like. I feel richer when I have a few things and lots of space available. I feel cluttered when I have lots of stuff. I also feel it's cosy to have great treasures I can rediscover. So feeling rich isn't everything. I'd rather be cosy than rich any time! And my ideal would be to put my treasures in really super treasure boxes. Lush.

When I lived in Kensington, in one of the most expensive parts of London just off the High Street, I detected a very interesting pattern of feeling poor. Since then I have observed it in many of my clients – and it matches up with the psychological studies made on consumer behaviour: when I feel poor, my craving for new things rises. Just in case you are wondering how on earth someone who felt so poor managed to live in the most expensive borough in London – that's one of my life's fun miracles. I have been very fortunate at times – though it wasn't all down to luck.

So imagine the struggling artist (whose eyes filled with tears when in London her cranberry juice cost twice as much as in Brighton) walking past the shops knowing she couldn't afford any of the nice things on view. Her money barely stretched to the essentials – you don't need to feel sorry for me, I felt sorry enough for myself to cover it! Because I knew I couldn't, and shouldn't, I wanted it even more. So I walked around with the thought "I really want this belt!" and it could become obsessive until I bought the belt (or whatever) or it would disappear from the shop window. I know I am not alone in giving in to the cravings and feeling really bad about it later.

It all stems from believing that our thoughts are real. Then I tried something different. I told myself that I could in fact buy whatever I wanted and allowed myself to go into all the shops looking for what I really, really wanted. What a surprise – I didn't feel so poor any more.

Feeling rich is about having choices and options.

I told myself if I really, really wanted something, I'd find a way to buy it but to my surprise there weren't many things I really wanted for long. The rule was to walk out of the shop and wait to see if I still wanted the item after three days or a week. If I still thought my life would be super-different through the purchase – fine, I'd buy it. Most of the time, the initial kick disappeared after a night. Most of the time the satisfaction of a buy wears off just as quickly, so I might as well save the cash.

Allowing yourself the possibility of buying what you want frees up good feelings. The 'never buy the first time you see it' philosophy really helps to differentiate what you want from an impulse buy. You will find more on impulse buying in the next chapter.

My best friend's partner was unemployed. With his self-esteem low and hopes dashed, he would complain about life in his local pub every evening. When my friend did the maths, she concluded that he could have £45 per week - about £195 a month or £2,340 per year and that could get you to the Maldives for a week - if he didn't spend it on beer every night. But he got furious. "With so little left in my life, the only thing left is my beer! You want to take my last enjoyment away from me?!" This attitude is widespread: because I can't afford the big good things, I might at least treat myself with small things. It all adds up.

When I have been around wealthy people, they seem to consume much less than the people who consider themselves not to be affluent. For me, being rich means being okay with being: not needing to consume all the time and not needing to spend all the time. It's very similar to the weight issue. Slim people don't need to eat so much; they are fine with sitting there not consuming a calorie. How many times a day do you spend a little money? On a coffee, small treats, little things? At a recent seminar it turned out that most of the people there spent around £5-£7 at Starbucks each day. To me that seemed far-fetched but who am I to argue with reality? How much do you spend on little extras per week?

Okay, if that hurt a bit, let me ask something more pleasant: what would you do with £1,000 if you had it in the bank? Did you know that all you need to do is save £2.73 each day and in one year you will have £1,000 - that's one Starbucks coffee approximately? Isn't that cool? Little numbers add up.

30. hey big SPENDER!

Spending Wisely - Whatever That Means

I'm hopeless
with money;
I simply spend
what i've got.

Freddie Mercury

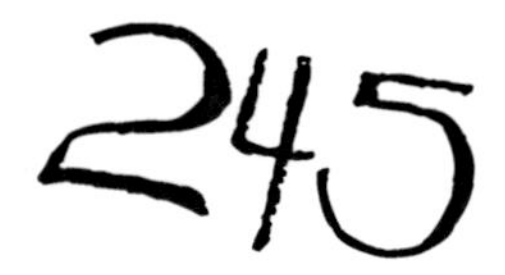

Can you walk into a shop, see something you absolutely love and leave without buying it – and still be completely happy? Do you use your money consciously or does it seem to run like sand through your fingers?

This chapter is about how you can spend wisely without boring yourself to death. When I hear the term 'spending wisely' it just doesn't sound like fun: imagining having more money to have fun with sounds much better. However, as we have already explored, money tends to stick with those who know how to handle it. In our sober moments of course we all know that we 'should' really think about how we are spending our cash – save some for a rainy day, not drink it away, not spend more than we have, be reasonable about it, blah blah blah. Gosh, even writing about it bores me!

On today's menu du jour, we have a fresh approach to the idea of growing your wisdom around money. Totally organic and accompanied with a side platter of sautéed fun tips and a mezze of games that help you create an honest and real menu of excellence. No more of this Budget Brûlée! Crème Brûlée, from which I derived this term, refers to the sugar crust on top which - when burnt correctly - becomes delicious caramel. However Budget Brûlée isn't just burning off some sugar, honey. It's more burning a big hole in your pocket/account/self-esteem. Delete as appropriate or add extra as needed.

One of the big issues Artistic Souls tend to face is – and I am not saying this is you of course – that we may be ever so slightly obsessive when we like something. It can go a bit like this: "I want it. I want it bad. I want it now. I should have it. I must have it. I love it! I deserve it. I'm worth it! I have to buy it! I can't afford it. I won't look. I will be alright. Oops, I am not, why did I do this, how did this happen? But I loved it so I had to buy it. It's not my fault. Oh, well. Argh, I am crap with money, I just need more."

So before we talk about any sensible things to do around spending wisely, I would like to point out the impulse imbroglio. Impulses are generally good things: we like acting on impulse because it feels alive and connected. When I was playing in the Frankfurt theatre, we were urged to act upon our impulse – in other words only react and start our lines when the real moment was right rather than say the lines when the other person finished speaking. The scene I shall never forget had my good friend and talented lead actor Daniel Kamen standing still for what felt like a lifetime. Not saying anything, not moving. After a long time, the director butted in: "What's going on, Daniel? Have you lost your words or your mind?" He just said, "I am waiting for the impulse".

We need to develop the sensitivity to feel the moment: to get the impulse, the intuitive feeling of when to strike. As a painter you may need the impulse that takes you from one brushstroke to the next, or as a musician you'd use your impulse to create more expression and hit the note just right, maybe even slightly off-beat but in-pulse. So we are quite attuned to a sudden hit of energy: a 'yes' energy that inspires us to move spontaneously.

When it comes to spending money, this hit of yes-energy can be a bit of a disaster for our well-meant ideas of being good and watching the money. We have so many good feelings anchored with acting on our impulse that it feels pretty gravitational to buy on impulse too.

But notice the distinction between impulse as in 'the real moment at which it is right' and impulse as in 'the sudden

wave of emotion', because this is where our own senses trick us. Unless you are a person whose impulse buys have proven to be the best – in which case ignore this part and continue as before.

This is not about being dogmatic and saying never to buy on impulse because it's bad. That sounds too one-way street to be a true solution. My observation is that buying on impulse, or indeed on any highly emotional state of mind, has led me to buy stuff that on reflection I wouldn't choose again. As our emotions go up, intelligence goes down and so the more excited I get about buying something, the more careful I am going to be about buying it right now.

Do you ever have buyer's remorse? Doubting your purchase in hindsight? If you do – you probably bought too quickly. Are you able to look at your bank statements regularly and agree with your spending? If not, you probably buy too quickly. Here is the ultimate method to enjoy the energy kick of the impulse and the freedom of choice:

Step 1: Look.
Step 2: Fall in love.
Step 3: Do not buy.

If you still want it after three days or a week, then you can go and buy it. You'll be surprised how much you can happily live without. It's just when we think "but I really need it now!" that it gets a bit intense. I remember 'needing' the new computer - right now. My old one was on the verge of giving up the ghost; everything would come to a halt if I didn't have a computer. My life would fall apart, I need it now! And yes, the new Apple Mac has just come out which is great timing.

But because I don't do quick shopping any more, I gave myself enough space to cool down and realise that a new Mac line means you can get the one from just before for much, much, less. So do I really need the latest model? Of course I'd really like it and I am genetically predisposed to be flashy. But actually, I can be very happy with the extra £500 saved.

It's when we attach the purchase to our happiness, the thought "Oh my, I can't live without that" that we mentally wrap ourselves into our own trap. Budget Brûlée made to order!

So what happens if the opportunity to buy is only here NOW? Let's say it's a sale and aren't sales a great opportunity for a BARGAIN? Personally I recommend passing sales items through the Fabulous Test. I ask:

1) Is it fabulous?
2) Will I think it's fabulous in a month/year?
3) Do I already have something similar?

Chances are if I love it a lot, especially clothes, it's another purple or turquoise top. Open my wardrobe and what do you find? Purple and turquoise tops.

Did you know that in the 1950s, German girls from good families were sent to Hausfrau school to learn how to run a household? One of the classes was on accounting because as a good German Hausfrau you needed to know how to buy all the food and goods the family need on your very tight budget. You needed to calculate well and precisely and no penny must be wasted. In a pre-credit world, what wasn't there could not be spent.

30. Hey Big Spender!
Spending Wisely - Whatever That Means

Not too long ago, they ran a series on German TV sending ladettes to the Hausfrau school, reconstructing the institution and teaching methods. It certainly made very interesting and entertaining TV drama. I watched the whole series on DVD whilst ironing. Spot the irony. I am glad times have moved on! Not just because I don't like ironing quite that much, and learning household accounting would not have harmed me or anyone I know – looking at the economy now it certainly looks like we missed that class! But times and the methods of teaching were more than a little harsher than today.

Most of us Artistic Souls don't have 'budgeting before buying' as a default setting. We tend to go about our ideas and daily business expecting money to be there, spend it as we see fit, and find ourselves surprised when we run out. "Where did it all go?" On the other hand, the idea of controlling our budgets, and spending more energy than necessary on money and tracking it, sounds worse than running out of it early, don't you think? If you are not sure what it is for you, check your bank account and the truth shall be revealed.

So what on earth can we do to make sure we are good with our money and don't have to monitor ourselves all the time? The answer is: set up **effective systems**. A system is a way of getting done what you actually want without having to make yourself go nuts over it. Once it's set up, you don't need to worry about the details of what it does any more.

Artrepreneur Principle 19:

Systems are consistent and free up our mental energy and time.

So let's roll up our sleeves, wash our hands and get started – metaphorically speaking. You don't actually need to wash your hands for this. But you do need to know what you are spending and what you really need to spend. So sit down and add up your numbers; you may have done this before in the Reality Checkmate game in chapter 21. If you have, just pull out your numbers and review them. If you haven't, this would be a perfect opportunity to do it. I am not going to stalk you. (Only in your dreams at night and you will love it.)

Basic fixed expenses like rent, transport and phone need to be calculated first. I like these bills to leave my account on the first three days of the month, so I know what I've got to work with within the first week. Because I like holidays and bigger things, I constantly need to save up. I can dream about being rich one day so I can buy a couch, or just save £50 a month and buy it next year. But have you noticed too that there is no £50 a month you can save at the end of the month? Or £300 or whatever amount you want to save? As good as I try to be, within three months something happens and the money is gone. Oops, I did it again. So here is where Evelyne's magical spending system idea comes in:

To make sure I am saving money every month, I set up a direct debit/standing order to my savings account that takes the money in the first week of every month. If I didn't have it set up as a standing order, I would most likely forget very quickly about my saintly intentions and say things like "I'll do it later. I have so many important things I need to do first." Maybe it's just me and hundreds of other people, maybe it's in the nature of the ever-inventive mind to lack consistency. That's why standing orders work magic. Once set up they run until further notice and I can go about my funny business and know that, in the background, it's all good.

Next up – household bookkeeping done for you!

Because monitoring yourself all the time is stupidly boring, I created a system to keep clarity about my spending:

- Set up different accounts with separate cards. You could either set up a separate bank account or apply for a credit card to put this into practice.
- Apart from your general main account, you could have a fun account on which you have your fun spending money – ideally with a bank card for that.

Because I wanted to really understand how much I needed for food and how to control my spending on this, I used a separate credit card for my food expenses. My pink card paid for everything food related because a) it was offered with good terms, b) I get extra vouchers for using it and c) it's pink!

Very importantly, the bill is set up to be paid in full by direct debit each month, so no credit card charges would ever apply. Basically it means that the credit card company is doing my personal bookkeeping for me at no cost. I just get a bill every month stating what I spent on food and drink. I promise you, I couldn't make it look so neat myself. After years of trying to track each purchase in account books or mobile phone applications I get one bill a month telling me exactly what's happened. With a separate account and card (from which you can take cash out and put it in a separate wallet) it's easy to track what your real numbers are. If you can't set up a separate account, just having a cash budget for going out can work too. But you will need that stylish extra wallet.

If you are in a so-called serious relationship (which I hope is less serious and more fun) and are sharing costs with your partner, it becomes more complicated. The best move ever for Thomas and me was to get married. I proposed that we have a 'Practical Marriage'; so I dressed up all in white, put a veil over my head and we turned up at Barclays Bank to open up a joint account. Isn't that romantic? There were no rings but we do both have a new, blue debit card. This is in addition to our personal accounts. So we each have our own money plus a common household account.

Speaking of marriage: instead of saying yes to each other in a ceremony and making all those vows, if they really want to show trust in one other in good times and in bad, why don't people simply exchange their personal pins?

Each month we transfer a regular payment to our joint account from which we now pay our rent and for food and some activities we do together (unless we have a date where I take him out or the other way around).

Gone are all the "but I bought this last time, so you should pay this and that". Gone are all the "I still owe you £13.24 but you paid for the petrol. That was £45.31 - ah, we'll do it later". I will always remember the young bike rental guy in Ecuador who had to pick us up because our quad bikes had broken down in the middle of nowhere. We chatted in the car and he was a newly-wed: eager to take care of his family but stressed because he didn't want to be greedy, but was very aware of the niggle between them when it came to who buys what. I taught him our joint account system and he nearly stopped driving to hug me. "You just saved my marriage! This is Genius!"

Okay, now that it's so much easier to oversee your spending and differentiate between where money goes out and for what, you can have a good hard look at your finances. There is no point telling yourself you need to cut costs when you don't really know what your costs are and why exactly. Think of a water tap. You can say, "I must save more water" and/or you can get one of those funny devices that let more air through than water, so you have less water pressure and use less water. But if you have a leak in the tap somewhere, you'll be wasting water no matter how good you are at holding back your personal usage.

That's why getting this beautiful overview about what goes out every month is important before you start fiddling with saving ideas. There is no reason for money diets: get rich by living poorly. With extreme mood swings and financial yo-yo effects as a free bonus. This is not what we are after.

As with many diets, money diets are more work than long-term results justify. It's all about living healthily.

To help you, I am devising a Budget Brûlée prevention programme and you can find full details of it on my website. Here is the practical application of it in a short and concise overview:

The Budget Brûlée prevention Programme:

Month 1

- Spending awareness.
- Set up accounts as applicable (fun/food/savings/household).

Month 2

- Watch the amounts being transferred and smile.
- If you have time left after that, enjoy the 'dreams costing' exercise.

Month 3:

- Set up spending and saving plan.
- Have a look at your actual spending in its various categories. Can you identify any leaks?

Month 4

- The creating game: write down a number you want to create (outside of your normal income) and brainstorm possibilities to do so. You will find more on this in chapter 32.

31. Selling Service,

Not Selling Your Soul

I put my heart
and my soul
into my work
and have
LOST MY MIND
in the process.

Vincent Van Gogh

One of the main challenges Artistic Souls face is that even though we may be desperate for money, we hate the idea of 'selling our soul' for it. But here's the good news: you cannot sell your soul. It's not up for sale! Nobody can actually take it and use it. Not in reality, only in your imagination.

Selling your soul means you don't love what you do in exchange for the money. It implies that exchanging your time purely for money has a negative effect on your mood and integrity. Which in turn affects our energy and general well-being. The overall feeling is that of submission to the necessity of making money. Which leaves you quite powerless and in pole position for being a victim. Being the creator of your wonderful life requires awakening to your choices because when you choose what you do, and the purpose you do things for, nobody can destroy your soul.

To test this out, I have personally gone from being a full-time artist to starting a career in the corporate world. I worked my way up from receptionist to international sales exec (with laptop and BlackBerry, oh yes!) in two years flat and my soul remained with me at all times, I promise. In fact I flourished as a person during this time. I was very aware that, for an artist, going into the real world to get a real job is a big deal. It can signify all sorts of failure scenarios from the dreaded resigning to 'reality' with a heavy sigh to the big no-no of 'giving up' – which you apparently must never ever do! Or else... or else... or else what?

Actually I did give up. I gave up on struggle. I don't care whether you should, or shouldn't, do that, I just did it. I had only started to learn about computers three years earlier and had plenty to catch up on. So I did. Instead of starting at 9am

I'd go in at 8:20am and do one of the Microsoft Office tutorials to learn about Excel and PowerPoint or Outlook. My acting background helped me keep my nerve in situations that could mildly be described as hairy – such as being asked to manage the diaries of the three Senior VPs and the Managing Director of the company during a busy trade show in New York. I had absolutely no idea what that meant, but I didn't want to sound like someone with no experience (which I was). I found that asking questions works wonders.

I also regularly got called into the boardroom when important board meetings were disrupted by malfunctioning technology. "Evelyne, can you make this work?" Evelyne stayed very calm and sorted it out, not showing that she had no clue whatsoever about such things and would normally have been described more as a technically challenged person than the office expert. But that's the power of acting for you. All that training had to pay off at some point!

When I was in the corporate world I wanted to learn the magic job: sales. It occurred to me that when you can sell, you will never be poor. Sales people are the first to be hired and the last to be fired. If you can sell, you will do swell. This is true for anyone. Now selling doesn't just mean products, it can be selling of ideas, selling of services or yourself as an artist/brand. The better you know how to present yourself, the higher your success rates.

However, for many Artistic Souls, the idea of selling in itself can be quite repellent. When we think of selling, as in 'trying to sneakily take money from someone else for some crap they don't need', then those with integrity and a heart of gold – as opposed to a wallet of gold – find it unethical to do. I remember that one time I was asked to lie to someone and

send some secret documents on, although we had promised not to. I was ready to quit my job that night and I was in tears until I was reassured the transaction was to help that person – and that was actually true. If selling means lying, stealing or scamming, and taking away from someone else, I am not interested. Sure, the idea is to create a result (i.e. money) but the way we go about it defines and distinguishes us. To me, there is much more to success than producing a result; it's also how you go about it. The end does not always justify the means. But selling doesn't mean all these bad things at all. Not by default!

Selling also means serving others in order to improve their life/business. All the things you buy and are happy with have been sold and I bet you didn't feel 'sold to' over them. On the contrary, aren't we glad when a good salesperson helps us make the right decision about a purchase? The joy of selling is to really serve another person and a really great sales person can advise you. They are not drooling just thinking about your cash. A great sales person doesn't need to put you under pressure or use psychological manipulation techniques. The top sales people are more interested in service than the sale. As my coach, the wonderful Rich Litvin, said, "Don't close the sale, open the relationship".

Would you be prepared to be a really good sales person? Someone who serves deeply in the world with the aim of creating win-win situations and serving others? If you do, you'll have a much better time and greater results especially in the long run. I am aware that there is sales training that is focused much more on short-term results and will have you think that as long as you get the money and you are selling something worthwhile it's okay to be 'creative' around your selling, meaning that white lies or spinning things is completely okay. This to me already smells of double standards and covering up hidden agendas. Why not lay the cards on the table and create trust? I believe that the short-sighted results-based 'instant success addiction' culture is what has brought our economy down, what stresses people and causes a lot of unhappiness in the world.

But serving people's needs and desires, offering good stuff in a cool way, that's a great thing. After all, your music wants to be heard and if nobody talks about it or makes it available, how can you have others sing along? We want excitement and entertainment in our lives and who doesn't like that being presented to them in an easy way? And that's what selling does: it gives you a chance to taste something new. Again there are great books and training for the idea of Selling by Giving, creating trust and relationships for sales. If selling is the thing you want to learn about, head over to the resources section for further information.

Steve Chandler says – and we'll use it as

Serve and you shall have.

Words of Gold, truly.

32. the Creating Game

I'm always thinking
about creating.
My future starts
when I wake up
every morning...
Every day I
find something
creative to do with

My Life.

Miles Davis

The cool thing about money is that it can be created. Unlike what we tend to think, you don't necessarily take anything away because you are adding economic value and money all the time.

How does that work? Think about it this way: if I give you a pound, and you give me one, we have one each. If I give you a giraffe and you give me a giraffe (another one), we each have a giraffe. But if I give you an idea and you give me an idea, we each have two ideas. Whereas before you had one, I had one, now we both have two. I love this. The power of creativity is such that it ADDS to the world and makes it a richer place.

Say I have a bookshelf that cost £30 to make. I buy some paint, sandpaper and a carving tool and I pay £30 for that. My balance sheet is now £60 so I sand down the shelf a bit, carve the most amazing design on it, paint it in ash-white with some granite underneath. I sand down some of the paint again so it looks 'shabby chic' and now it is very sexy and I've seen shelves in that style go for £300 on eBay and in shops for more than that.

It's definitely going to sell for much more than the £60 that it has as cost price, right? Say it goes for £250. Let's do the maths: £250 - £60 = £190 and that £190 of value was just created by me. It didn't exist before. I had an old pine bookshelf worth £30 that may have sold for £20 as it's not new and it wasn't anything special. But now it's definitely worth at least £250; it's one of a kind and it's fancy so why on earth am I even selling it? It's so nice! Also the guy who sold me the paint and tools made £30 and is a very happy man today. It could be a woman but in my mind for some odd reason it's a very handsome man with extremely good customer service skills. So really £220 was created: £190 went to me and £30 to my handsome DIY seller.

Money is added value. If you make a music album, whatever the value of the album will be wasn't there before! Imagine Beyoncé, who sold many millions of albums and made millions of dollars from it. These multimillions of value didn't exist before she made the album. The money may have existed but the 'worth' of this album didn't. So how can you create money? By adding something of value that someone else is happy to pay for. This can be your acting, teaching, painting shelves, translating; people have businesses making birthday cards or walking dogs, anything that is of service to someone else is bound to be a source of money to you.

So, let's brainstorm all sorts of ways in which you could create money. Write down all ideas, bad or good and even the horrid ones because creativity knows no judgement.

Exercise:

Write down your ideas of how you could be of service and add value in the world. If you'd like this as a beautiful worksheet, please download ours form www.artrepreneurbook.com

1) ______________________________

____

____

2) ______________________________

____

____

3) ______________________________

____

____

4) ______________________________

____

____

5) ______________________________

____

____

6) ______________________________

____

____

7) ______________________________

____

____

8) ______________________________

____

____

9) ______________________________

____

____

10) ______________________________

____

____

33. How Bad Is Debt?

If you owe the
bank $100 that's
your problem.
If you owe the
bank $100 million,
that's the
bank's
problem

J. Paul Getty

33. How Bad Is Debt?

I was at one of my many training courses. The trainer talked about the stuff I already knew and agree with: yes, life is great when you are courageous; no, I don't want to be mediocre; yes, I am ready to stand up for my greatness; no, I am not going to go back to my old habits. But I knew by that time that these things are easier said than done. I experienced a great high at seminars and when I got back home the effects of the seminars washed away like footprints in the sand.

What could make my decision to nurture my power practical and a day-to-day thing?

I knew I needed someone in my life to hold me to it, to help me lift and take action from that powerful place in me I had unveiled again and again during seminars and seemed to lose when on my own in my room thinking 'what next?' I decided I was going to work with the best coaches in the world to turn what I 'know' into what I really live. For me, the best coach I knew was Michael Neill: I loved his work and approach and the 'non-salesy' style. I contacted him and decided to invest in working with him. Needless to say this Supercoach[19], who is working with Hollywood celebs as well as business people, had published books and has a radio show and was charging far more than I had in my savings. So in theory it was not possible to work with him.

I grew up having learnt that you mustn't get into debt because once you are in debt you are in big trouble that spirals out of control. You must only spend what you have, or ideally less. The big D-word (Debt) was to be avoided at all costs so I

---

19 Visit the Supercoach Academy at www.supercoach.com for information about Michael's coaching training. My recommendation is the book *Supercoach*.

couldn't afford Michael Neill. End of story.

Beginning of reality: I decided to go with what I wanted (rather than what I thought I could have) and make the impossible possible. I wanted to make a leap and that leap required a high investment so I took out a credit card loan. I'd never done that before. It was a lot of work for me to compare the cards, apply for all sorts of cards, and read the small print and, yes, I got it wrong and ended up paying more than I had planned for. The card also helped pay for some more training. My reasoning: if this coaching stuff works, surely I'd be making the money back in no time! Admittedly, I felt quite sheepish about it all because debt really was the forbidden path for me. So my father mustn't know. Shhhhh!

Interestingly, nothing bad happens when you're in debt. Yes, they can take your house away when you don't pay up but it takes a long time to get to that (apart from the fact you need a house to lose). Usually debt just means you need to pay something back. Generally we can do this over time but the psychological stress I have witnessed in people far outweighs the real situation. Debt doesn't hurt. It just means we owe money. Only money. We still have all our human rights, our dignity, our ability to make free choices. Our relationships, our friends, our things.

The tricky thing with credit cards and loans of course is the way in which debt mounts up, so of course we want to avoid the mountain getting too big. Paying off what you can each month is important. Gosh, that is such basic stuff, I'm sure you know that. The problem isn't that we don't know what's right, it's more that we like to close our eyes to it. What I want here is to bring in a little ease around the D-word. We tend to stress ourselves about it more than does anyone

any good. To be in integrity and true to our word, I think it's important to pay off your debt. There is a lot to be said for living debt-free, but I will point out that the richest people and businesses in the world are often in debt. In a way it's more about being at peace with your situation that makes all the difference, not the situation itself.

A few months after I took out the loan, I had a chat about spending money with my wonderful dad. He introduced me to one of his really useful distinctions that made all the sense in the world: spending money you don't have on things that don't last is stupid. Foolish people do it and it's why they end up in big trouble. Going on holidays and shopping sprees in Barcelona, buying TVs or cars is what gets people into the downward spiral of debt. But investing money in your education and development is a wise thing to do (see chapter 25) and even borrowing money to be able to do so is a good idea. Because money invested in your education helps you generate more (and helps you get the jobs you really want). So it's a good thing.

34. the golden compass

I've lost money and made money, but I know my

WAY AROUND

financially.

Jack Nicholson

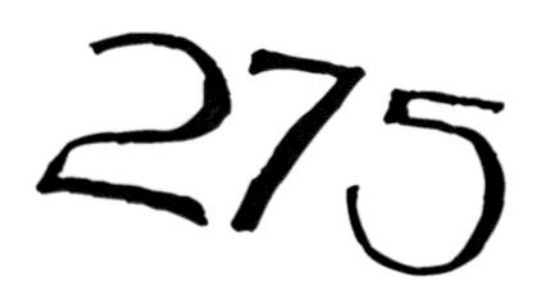

In the book and film *The Golden Compass* the lead character Lyra journeys to the north pole to save the children that have mysteriously gone missing. She has to find her way through a world of deceit and betrayal, conspiracies and secret plans and is given a golden compass, which allows her to read the truth behind all the stories and words of the adults around her. When it comes to money, advice varies greatly and our attitude and motivation may fluctuate, too. Wouldn't it be great to have a golden compass of our own to find out what's what and separate the truth from the talk?

Some teaching suggests you should visualise yourself attracting money, gives you exercises to be grateful for your bills or has you pinning up cheques with your name and the amount of money you wish to receive on your fridge. Does it work? I am not aware of scientific studies proving this, but I am aware that people who long for more money and find it hard to break their lazy habits around money prefer a philosophy of wishful thinking to practical common sense action. Throughout human history you can find that where we have a lack of understanding we replace it with superstitious beliefs. Whether I perform a rain dance around money or not is unlikely to really affect my income (unless I create a show out of it and charge and then get a range of licensed 'rain dance money magnet' products going that happen to sell well).

A golden compass would tell you that the rain dance for money is not the reason for your pay cheque, but that dancing in the rain is a wonderful thing and very refreshing. Refreshed and liberated people could possibly find it easier to go out and create money, adding value to the world. So the rain dance has its place.

The cheque on the fridge is not the solution, but if a cheque on your fridge helps you remember your goal, it's a great idea.

I had a nice coffee with my mum in Christopher Square in London. The Christmas lights were illuminating Oxford Street and the Italian biscuit selection was just what made a post-Christmas shopping afternoon perfect. As we chatted, Mum admitted she still had fears around running out of money even though her financial adviser kept telling her she could relax. My coaching ears pricked up. It turns out she found it easy to relax when she knew 'for sure' that she was fine, in other words when she knew how much she actually had. When the numbers were blurry and unspecific, her fears and concerns crept back in. The only reason for her to really get afraid was when she didn't know what to do, which made her feel helpless and powerless. I gave my mum a golden compass, which for her was her bank and investment statements. She can use her golden compass to eliminate her confusion and fears, find direction and her truth and the security she's looking for. If her numbers are low, she needs to get her act together and create more opportunities to sell her paintings. If her numbers are okay, she can still create more but she doesn't have to do it out of need.

We all have a golden compass of truth – and many of us don't use it. If Lyra didn't use her golden compass, she would have bought into the stories misguiding her and probably would have ended up locked up at the North Pole. We all would have missed out on the transformation from the depressed to empowered ice bear.

Life has many depressed ice bears and waiting for us to liberate them. Our dreams and childlike imagination wants to run free and not be locked up in the dark. Use your golden compass. What's yours?

35. SOOOO...

There is a certain combination of

ANARCHY

and discipline in the way I work.

Robert de Niro

So let me summarise all we've gone through in *The Artrepreneur*:

- Artistic Souls more or less live out a preconditioning of the belief that art comes with no money and that struggle is part of the process.
- We find ourselves with a fluctuating or non-existent financial love life.
- We can shift into a much more useful and powerful world view of knowing that money and inspiration are abundantly available to us through taking clear and consistent action without the bad thoughts around it.

Artrepreneur Principle 1

The way we think about our world defines its borders. We want to recognise and celebrate the borders of our world and g(r)o(w) beyond them.

- We either master money or let money be the master of us. Mastering money means mastering the categories of making money, keeping money and spending/investing it.
- To change our behaviour and attitude towards money, we want to enhance our relationship with it.
- We recognise our limitations through feeling stuck or not achieving a desired result. We don't have to control, nor

do we need to change the world, we merely concentrate on creating what we want to see in the world.

- Our main problem with money is the meaning we attach to it.

Artrepreneur Principle 2

The problem with money is not that we do or don't have it. It's how we feel about having or not having it.

- Our feelings about money are based on our stories, whether they are real or born out of our assumptions.

Artrepreneur Principle 3

Money is man's best friend. But you've got to tame your thoughts around it.

- Like a dog your thoughts around money can either run berserk or be a loyal companion in your quest for a good life.

Our greatest weaknesses hold within them the seed of our greatest strength.

- Our greatest weakness gives us a strong reason to develop a deep interest in the subject, which may later become our greatest strength. Many experts know so much about their chosen field because it used to be their greatest challenge.

You have your money story and your money history. Both are only stories. One current. One past.

- You don't need to cling to your stories. In other words you can write your own empowering one.
- You have the opportunity to turn your story around and become the hero in your own movie; there are definitely vacancies for modern-day inspirations.

Money doesn't have power. You have power.

- Money doesn't make the world go around. People do.
- For us to be truly financially free, we want to liberate ourselves from our emotional attachment to money.
- We like having the power. Creativity is power. The power to create in the world.

Money is a trading tool.

- We don't get upset about hammers or spades. Let's keep it cool with money.
- Money can be made where value is added.
- Money is a form of exchange that is easier to take around than giraffes.

Artrepreneur Principle 8

Money doesn't mean anything unless you make it mean something.

- Money itself has no meaning until we give it meaning. It's not 'bad' in itself, it just is what it is. Humans are the meaning makers and we don't have to make money a mean or unkind thing.
- You are a worthy human being no matter how much money you have, no matter how big your hammer.
- You don't have to attach your personal happiness to the bone of achievement – it's optional.

Artrepreneur Principle 9

Creating your dreams is powerful. Living in a dream is powerless.

- There is no need to wait for salvation. It's powerless and boring.
- Glass slippers are hazardous.
- The best awakening is the one to your own power.

Money isn't always in what you do. But it's certainly not in what you don't do.

- Be visionary. Be bold. You might as well.
- Just because there is no market doesn't mean you couldn't grow one.
- The money isn't in what *you* do; it's in what people are willing to pay for.

Success is Succession.

- Success is not a quick fix. It's based on the layers of your past actions and experience.
- Most 'overnight success' stories have a history of a decade or more behind them.
- Success grows organically one layer at a time. Focus on each layer and you'll cultivate a strong foundation.

Artrepreneur Principle 12

You don't work as hard as you can but as hard as you think.

- Hard no. 1 is "Oh, I hate it, it's terribly hard".
- Hard no. 2 is working hard for a worthy goal whether you feel like it in the moment or not. That is what successful people do.
- Hard no. 3 is indulging yourself with the image of working hard. "Look how cool I am sacrificing my life for this work. I am bleeding for this with passion." It's a fashion and it's impractical.
- How we perceive our efforts determines how 'hard' we really work – inside our head as opposed to in the 'real world'.

Artrepreneur Principle 13

Making money from what you love is based on the sweet spot encompassing what you love and what other people pay for.

- Find out what you love to do.
- Research what people are happy to pay for.
- Find the sweet spot of common denominators.

Fees hold no meaning. They are simply numbers.

- Just like telephone numbers, we don't need to beat around the bush with our fees.
- You can set your fees based on market research, heart-based and guided by your personal truth. Or a powerful combination of the two.
- Fees are set according the value we deliver, the market we are targeting, and the lifestyle we choose.

We are motivated by meaning. Let's make the numbers mean something really cool.

- We want to find a reason to make money. It will keep us motivated for longer.
- Find your three magic numbers:

  1) What you need to survive.
  2) What you can live with.
  3) What makes for an amazing life!

The magic of transformation lies in deep care.

- There are behaviours that support our growth and evolution and others that stand firmly in the way of effortless success.
- Love is the key to transformation.

Worry is worry no matter how much money you have.

- Worry always finds a way to creep up whether about money or anything else.

- Worry is imagination turned against us. To stop worrying does not mean to stop taking action or caring.
- Even millionaires are known to worry about money.

Making money is a skill, not a coincidence.

- Hanging cheques on your fridge or dreaming about attracting money can be fun, but should never replace using your brain and taking action.
- When you get into your 1,000-ideas phase then write them down.

Systems are consistent and free up our mental energy and time.

- Because we love using our time to do constructive and creative things we can use systems.
- Once set up, they regularly perform a wanted task

such as transferring money to a savings account without us having to actively do it over and over again.

Serve and you shall have.

- We don't have to sell our soul to make money.
- We don't have to sell using a 'taking' energy.
- Being authentic and caring beings, we can shift into service, which is of more use to everyone.

Afterword

I sincerely hope to have served you deeply and that you had some fun on the way.

If you are happy with this book, I would be thrilled if you could let me and the world know by posting a review or comment on my website www.artrepreneurbook.com and, very importantly, on Amazon! Feel free to tweet, Facebook and chat about it (# artrepreneur). That's how we get the word out and make sure more Artistic Souls are become powerfully liberated ice bear heroes.

PS: Make sure to live happily ever after.

With love, smiles and warm greetings from the giraffes.

Resources

Time sweetening crossword puzzle – solution:

1↓: Question word about an object: What
2↓: Opposite of off: on
3→: Our planet: earth
4↓: Conjugation of 'to be' second person singular: are
5→: What you say to a person talked to directly in three letters: you
6→: The equivalent of taking action: doing

Y 5→	O 2↓	U	W 1↓	
A 4↓	N		H	
R	■	■	A	
E 3→	A	R	T	H
D 6→	O	I	N	G

References

Baker, Dan, ***What Happy People Know***

Chandler, Steve, ***9 lies that hold your business back***

---------------------***17 Lies that Hold you Back (and the truth that will set you free)***

---------------------***100 Ways be Wealthy***

---------------------***Fearless***

---------------------***Reinventing Yourself***

---------------------***The Joy of Selling***

---------------------***The Story of You***

---------------------***The Woman who Attracted Money***

---------------------***Time Warrior***

Coelho, Paolo***, The Winner Stands Alone***

Covey, Stephen R, ***The 7 Habits of Highly Effective People***

Dwoskin, Hale, ***The Sedona Method***

Dyer, Dr Wayne, www.drwaynedyer.com

Eden, Darren www.darreneden.com

Frederick , Shane and Loewenstein, George, "Hedonic Adaptation" in Daniel Kahneman, Ed Diener and Norbert Schwarz (eds), ***Scientific Perspectives on Enjoyment, Suffering and Well-Being.***

Fritz, Robert, ***The Path Of Least Resistance***

Guillebeau, Chris, ***279 Days to Overnight Success***

Holden, Robert, PhD ***Success Intelligence***

Katie, Byron, ***Loving what is***

Sonja Lyubormirsky, ***The How of Happiness***

McKenna, Paul, ***I Can Make You Rich***
Neill, Michael, ***Feel Happy Now***
------------------ ***Supercoach***
------------------- ***You can have what you want***
Seligman, Martin, ***Learned Optimism***
Shimoff, Marci, ***Happy For No Reason***
---------------------***Love For No Reason***
Tolle, Eckhart, ***The Power of Now***;
see also www.eckharttolle.com
Watzlawick, Paul, ***The Pursuit of Unhappiness***
Whetten, Brian, ***Selling by Giving*** (audio course)

Websites

- My website where you can download audio courses including ***The Curse of Creativity*** www.brinkcoaching.co.uk
- See also www.artrepreneurbook.com where you will find more resources, people to help you in your business, worksheets and details of the Budget Brûlée programme
- Clay Collins: www.marketingshow.com
- Chris Gillebeau: chrisguillebeau.com
- Paul Grignon film, ***Money as Debt***, which explains the history of our money system: www.youtube.com/watch?v=Dc3sKwwAaCU
- Michael Jordan advert: www.youtube.com/watch?v=m-EMOb3ATJ0
- Danny McAskill and his bike tricks: www.youtube.com/watch?v=Z19zFlPah-o
- Michael Neill's Supercoach Academy: www.supercoach.com
- Brian Whetten, Selling by Giving course and audios: www.sellingbygiving.net

Just to be future-proof: as website links change, please do not feel deterred if one link won't work. Just type in the titles into google or youtube and I am sure you'll find what we're talking about here.

About the Author

Evelyne Brink is a Success Coach for Artistic Souls (from small business owners with big visions to fully blown artists) using her insightful creativity to help her clients gain recording contracts, pay rises, customers and awards. They also experience a rise in their quality of life and levels of happiness experiencing a deeper understanding and love for themselves and others.

Before taking up coaching, she was internationally renowned as a singer (Sony Music, Zyxx Music), songwriter (aka Diva Eve) and comedienne performing her one woman shows from NY to Berlin, London to Edinburgh as well as touring the globe as Europe's leading Madonna Impersonator (as seen on TV).

She lives with her wonderful partner Thomas in London. At the time of publishing she is expecting her first child.

Her passion is enabling people to live their individual life and be true to their deepest values. She enjoyed writing this piece about herself in third person as it makes her feel somehow royal.

She also likes giraffes.

Lightning Source UK Ltd.
Milton Keynes UK
UKOW030752101012

200334UK00001B/30/P